Resurrection Lifestyle

Experience the
Extraordinary Power
Jesus Intended for You

Resurrection Lifestyle

*Experience the
Extraordinary Power
Jesus Intended for You*

BY

JOSEPH MORRIS

Harrison House
Tulsa, Oklahoma

Table of Contents

Introduction

I feel like the prophet Joel when he said, *"Blow ye the trumpet in Zion, and sound an alarm in my holy mountain: let all the inhabitants of the land tremble: for the day of the LORD cometh, for it is nigh at hand"* (Joel 2:1). I am sounding an alarm. My call as an end-time preacher is to wake people up everywhere and get them to realize that Jesus is coming back soon.

As I travel around the world, my messages are always delivered with a sense of urgency. I want Christians to realize that it is time to start doing what they were called to do and live a resurrection lifestyle by walking in the power of God before the return of the Lord.

It's time for that power to flow *through* Christians and not just *to* them. We are moments away from His return and only have a small window of opportunity to get the job done.

Jesus is not coming back for a church that is living below its potential. No, He expects us to be demonstrating the power and anointing of God the same way the early church did.

Most Christians today are not sharing the Gospel with their family, friends, coworkers, and neighbors, let alone laying hands on the sick and seeing the power of God manifest. Why? They do not realize the power that lies within them.

Demonstrating the Power of God

Before Jesus ascended into heaven, He gave the church an assignment, which was to go into the entire world and preach the Gospel. However, He did not leave the church powerless when He left. The Holy Spirit was sent to live in us; and believers were promised that when they preached in the name of Jesus, He would confirm what they said with signs and wonders. The sick would be healed, demons would be cast out, and the dead would be brought back to life. (Mark 16:15-20.)

Imagine what would happen if Christians began to function in their fullest potential and allowed the power of God to flow through them. There would be a marked difference between those who know the Lord and those who do not. You can be sure the unsaved would flock to those who could demonstrate the power of God. The closer we get to the return of the Lord, the crazier this world is going to get. Nonbelievers are going to search for answers, and we need to be a beacon of light that will draw them to Christ.

When you become born again, your life should change. People should be able to tell that something is different about you. Second Corinthians 5:17 says, *"if any man be in Christ, he is a new creature: old things are passed away; behold, all things are become new."* The apostle Paul understood this when he prayed for the church at Ephesus. He wanted them to know who they were in Christ.

Wherefore I also, after I heard of your faith in the Lord Jesus, and love unto all the saints, Cease not to give thanks for you, making mention of you in my prayers; That the God of our Lord Jesus Christ, the Father of glory, may give unto you the spirit of wisdom and revelation in the knowledge of him: The eyes of your understanding being enlightened; that ye may know what is the hope of his calling, and what the riches of the glory of his inheritance in the saints, And what is the exceeding greatness of his power to us-ward who believe, according to the working of his mighty power…And hath put all things under his feet, and gave him to be the head over all things to the church, Which is his body, the fulness of him that filleth all in all.

EPHESIANS 1:15-23

Notice verse 23 says that we are the "fullness of Christ." We are not a fragment, or a small portion of Jesus; we are the fullness of Him. Jesus said in John 14:9, *"…he that hath seen me hath seen the Father."* Now let me ask you this. When people look at you, what do they see? Do they see Jesus? The apostle John said that if you say that

Christ dwells in you, you should walk like Him. (1 John 2:6.) If you are not walking the way Jesus did, then what is on the inside of you? I would say you are filled with religious tradition instead of the resurrection power of Jesus Christ.

Being God Inside-Minded

You may want to live a resurrection lifestyle but wonder how you can get started. To begin manifesting the power of God in your life, you first have to change your way of thinking. Instead of thinking that you could never be used in the gifts of the Spirit, you have to remember who dwells in you. When you know who you are in Christ, you won't hesitate to lay hands on the sick and command devils to leave.

The more you meditate on who you are in Christ, the easier it will be to step out in the things of God. One of your biggest enemies will be religion. It will try to hold you back in the things of God, especially in the move of the Spirit. Realize that you are not alone in fighting religion. The apostles battled religious tradition all the time. But as they magnified the name of Jesus, they were able to cut through the religious tradition; and God was able to demonstrate His power.

The apostles were ordinary men without any formal religious training. Yet, because of the time they spent with Jesus, they were able to turn the world upside down (Acts 17:6) after He ascended into heaven. It wasn't with "excellence of speech" or their college degrees that they were able to accomplish this feat.

Acts 4 records the arrest of Peter and John after a lame man was healed at the Temple gate called Beautiful. When the two men were brought before the High Priest, he demanded to know *"...By what power, or by what name, have ye done this?"* (Acts 4:7). Peter, being filled with the Holy Spirit, boldly answered the High Priest's charges. The scripture then says, *"Now when they saw the boldness of Peter and John, and perceived that they were unlearned and ignorant men, they marveled; and they took knowledge of them, that they had been with Jesus"* (v. 13).

There is something about the anointing of God. It does not matter who the messenger is. When the power of God comes on you, you are turned into another man or woman. That day, these unlearned fishermen caused approximately 5,000 men to believe on the name of Jesus. (Acts 4:4.) It was the power of God that got the people's attention. It was not the apostle's great oratory skills that brought this many people to the Lord. It was the anointing of God.

We never see anywhere in the Bible that people thought Jesus was a great preacher. What caused them to

sit up and listen was the power and authority in which He taught. In fact, *"they were astonished at his doctrine: for he taught them as one that had authority, and not as the scribes"* (Mark 1:22).

Clothed in the Power of God

Anointing and authority are synonymous. Jesus was anointed and the power of God was there to back Him up. John said, *"...as he is, so are we in this world"* (1 John 4:17). That means we are supposed to be like Jesus while we are here on the earth. Jesus only did and said what the Father told Him to do and say. He demonstrated God in the earth, and He wants us to demonstrate Him.

Before Jesus ascended into heaven, He told the disciples to tarry in Jerusalem until they were endued with power from on high. (Luke 24:49.) Basically, he told them to wait in Jerusalem until they were clothed from heaven. I like to explain His instructions like this.

Most of my ministry is in the United States. During the times that I travel overseas to minister, I rarely get to do any sightseeing. I go to a country to minister and that is where my focus is. However, one time when I was in London, I decided I wanted to look at some suits. I went to one particular store and asked the owner, "What makes your suits better than anybody else's?"

He pointed to my right shoulder and asked me what happened. I explained that I injured my shoulder while playing football many years ago. He told me that he would add a little extra padding to the right shoulder. That way both shoulders would look even. He would also tuck in both armholes in a particular way that would make me look taller and thinner.

I thought, *Man, if you can pull this off, I will buy all my suits from you!* You see, I've been growing all my life, just not up. I have always been the proper weight. I've just never been the proper height to match my weight!

This tailor was able to hide my frailties and faults, and that is exactly what happens when you are baptized in the Holy Spirit. You become clothed with the power and anointing of God. Nobody is perfect. In spite of our imperfections, the Holy Spirit enables us to walk in the power of God and to demonstrate Christ on the earth.

If your coworker showed up in the office wearing dirty pants, each pant leg was a different length, and his wrinkled and equally soiled shirt was not tucked inside his pants, you would wonder what was wrong with the guy. You would probably think that he had a little too much to drink the night before.

Nobody seems to notice when we are not dressed right spiritually. In fact, Christians make excuses for wearing things like fear, anger, bitterness, etc. In Matthew 22 Jesus

tells the parable of the wedding banquet. A king prepared a feast for his son's wedding. The invitations had been sent out but nobody came.

The king then told his servants to go out into the highways and invite anyone they found. One man showed up to the wedding reception not clothed properly. The king asked him, *"Friend, how comest thou in hither not having a wedding garment?"* (v. 12). The king then had the man thrown out of the banquet. It was not okay that he was not dressed properly.

It is not okay when Christians walk around spiritually underdressed. They have been invited to demonstrate the power of God to the world; but they are weak in their faith, spend little or no time in prayer, and rarely read their Bibles. They are quick to pass off their ineffectiveness by saying, "Oh, well. We're just not doing what we're supposed to be doing." They allow fear to hold them back from doing the greater works Jesus talked about in John 14. They are more concerned about what people will think than pleasing God.

I want to encourage you to clothe yourself in the supernatural equipment that is available to believers everywhere. It's time for Christians to walk in the same authority and miraculous power that Jesus did. I want to inspire and instruct you on how to break free from the mediocrity of ineffective religious rituals and tap into an

over-the-top, vibrant quality of life in God through a resurrection lifestyle.

Fasten your seatbelts; you are about to begin a fantastic journey. The Holy Spirit will have you doing things and going places that you never dreamed of. As you begin walking down the road of the supernatural, you will not only please God, you will also transform the lives of everyone you meet.

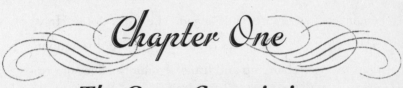

Chapter One

The Great Commission

*B*efore Jesus ascended into heaven, His instructions to the early church were pretty clear: Preach the good news of the kingdom to men everywhere. He wanted them to continue doing the works that He did while He was on the earth. That meant they needed to allow the power of God to flow through them to destroy the works of the devil by laying hands on the sick, casting out devils, and raising the dead.

Before they got started, Jesus told them to stay in Jerusalem until they were clothed in His power. Aren't you glad that God never assigns you with a task without first giving you the necessary equipment to complete it? God knew that the disciples could not change the world in their own strength. They needed a helper, so He endued them with Himself to get the job done.

He did this by pouring out the Holy Spirit—also known as the Comforter, Counselor, Helper, Advocate, Intercessor, Strengthener, and Standby (John 14:26 AMP)—to take up residence inside of them. In a small upper room where 120 men and women had gathered, the Holy Spirit descended on them on the day of Pentecost. Their lives were forever changed. The work of the Holy Spirit did not stop there. He has been active throughout the centuries changing and transforming the lives of ordinary men and women and enabling God to do extraordinary exploits through them.

Getting Drunk Before Noon!

When the apostles and the 120 were baptized in the Holy Spirit that day, Jerusalem was filled with Jews from every nation celebrating Shavuot, or the Feast of Weeks. This Jewish holiday commemorates the giving of the Torah at Mount Sinai. Shavuot occurs 50 days after the first day of Passover and is sometimes known as Pentecost, a Greek word meaning "the holiday of 50 days."

The streets soon became crowded with people when they heard the sound of the violent wind that filled the house this small gathering was staying in. When the apostles tried to explain what had happened, the Jews became more bewildered because each person heard them speak in their native languages. Some people in the crowd began to make fun of them and accused them of being drunk. Peter responded to their coarse accusations:

For these are not drunken, as ye suppose, seeing it is but the third hour of the day. But this is that which was spoken by the prophet Joel; And it shall come to pass in the last days, saith God, I will pour out of my spirit upon all flesh: and your sons and your daughters shall prophesy, and your young men shall see visions, and your old men shall dream dreams: and on my servants and on my hand-maidens I will pour out in those days of my spirit; and they shall prophesy."

ACTS 2:15-18

John 16:8 (NKJV) says that the Holy Spirit will convict the world of sin. As the people in Jerusalem listened to Peter that morning, their hearts were pricked. The number of men and women who believed on the name of Jesus and were added to the kingdom that day totaled 3,000.

From these verses, we also see how God wanted the Holy Spirit to be poured out. Many people errantly think that the power of God is only for those who are in the five-fold ministry. We don't see that here at all. Verse 17 clearly says that God will pour out His Spirit on *all* flesh. That means everybody, including you. As a result of being filled with the Holy Spirit, our sons and daughters will prophesy, young men will see visions, and old men will dream dreams. Whether you are young or old, male or female, you are included in the outpouring of the Holy Spirit.

This was not a one-time incident. The baptism of the Holy Spirit has been continually poured out throughout the

ages on anybody who desires it. On the day of Pentecost, the Holy Spirit descended in what appeared to be flames of fire. Today, we receive the Holy Spirit through the laying on of hands. It's just as easy for us to receive the infilling of the Spirit today as it was then. We do not have to tarry for it as it was once taught; we only have to ask for it by faith.

God's Mercy Poured Out

Why is the infilling of the Holy Spirit so important to Christians nowadays? We are standing at the edge of eternity and are only moments away from the Rapture of the church. God wants to manifest Himself in ways that have not been seen since the start of the church age. That will only happen when ordinary Christians yield to the Holy Spirit and allow His power to flow through them to minister to those around them.

There are more people living on the earth now than there has been since the beginning of time. God wants to make sure that as many people as possible are part of the Rapture. After the church is gone, the Great Tribulation begins. We are in that small sliver of time when God's mercy will be poured out on mankind before the final judgment of the world.

We have seen throughout the Bible that God's mercy has always preceded judgment. Noah preached for 120 years before the Flood destroyed mankind. The angels delivered Lot and his family from Sodom and Gomorrah before God's wrath hit those cities. Before the return of Jesus, God's mercy will once again be poured out on the earth. And since the body of Christ is God's representatives on the earth, that mercy will be manifested through us.

The question is: Are you ready to be God's instrument?

Preparing the Disciples

As Jesus was eating the Passover meal with His disciples—His last meal before going to the Cross—He began to share with them the things that would shortly take place. He wanted to encourage them so when He was arrested, they would have the strength to endure. He also had to prepare them for the task they would have to complete after He was crucified and ascended into heaven. But that evening, they could not comprehend that they would have to give birth to the church and that God Himself would dwell inside of them.

Jesus told them He was going away for a while and that they did not need to be troubled. He had to leave to prepare a place for them so one day they could be together again. Then He said something that totally puzzled them. *"And whither I go ye know, and the way ye know"* (John 14:4). Can you imagine how upset and confused the disciples

probably felt? While they believed that Jesus was the Messiah, they also believed that He was going to set up His Messianic kingdom in Jerusalem. They could not understand why Jesus would leave them now. Plus, He told them that they knew how to get where He was going.

They were shaking their heads saying, "No, Lord, we don't know what You're talking about." Did you ever notice that Jesus had a way of talking to His disciples that often left them clueless? He responded, *"I am the way, the truth, and the life: no man cometh unto the Father, but by me. If ye had known me, ye should have known my Father also: and from henceforth ye know him, and have seen him"* (vv. 6,7).

Unfortunately, His answer didn't help them much. They still didn't know what He was talking about. Philip was the brave one who further questioned Jesus by asking, "Well, Lord, if You will just show us who the Father is then we'll be satisfied." (v. 8.)

Have you also noticed how the disciples easily exasperated Jesus? I can imagine Him wondering, *Where have they been for the last three years? Weren't you there, Philip, when Peter declared that I was the Christ, the son of the Living God?* (Matt. 16:13-16.) He testily replied,

> *Have I been so long time with you, and yet hast thou not known me, Philip?...the words that I speak unto you I speak not of myself: but the Father that dwelleth in me, he*

doeth the works. Believe me that I am in the Father, and the
Father in me: or else believe me for the very works' sake."

JOHN 14:9-11

Being Filled With God

They needed to understand that Jesus was able to do
what He did because God was in Him. If that was too
much for them to comprehend, then Jesus asked that they
at least believe Him because of the works He performed.
Surely they could believe He was the Son of God because
of the people who had been healed, delivered, and raised
from the dead. They needed to understand this because in a
short period of time, the God who created the universe was
going to take up residence in them so they could begin
what we now call the church.

Only moments before Jesus went to the Cross, He told
His staff that they were going to have to duplicate the
works that He did. He said:

> *He that believeth on me, the works that I do shall he do*
> *also; and greater works than these shall he do…And what-*
> *soever ye shall ask in my name, that will I do, that the*
> *Father may be glorified in the Son. If ye shall ask any*
> *thing in my name, I will do it.*

JOHN 14:12-14

Earlier in His ministry, Jesus sent the disciples out two by two to lay hands on the sick and to cast out devils. (Mark 6:6-13.) Although they had great success on this outing, they were not always successful in getting good results. Only a few chapters later, we see that they could not cast the devil out of a young boy. (Mark 9:18.) Maybe Jesus knew they were wondering how they were going to do "greater" works when He said:

> *I will pray the Father, and he shall give you another Comforter, that he may abide with you for ever; Even the Spirit of truth; whom the world cannot receive, because it seeth him not, neither knoweth him: but ye know him; for he dwelleth with you, and shall be in you."*

> JOHN 14:16,17

I'm sure the disciples thought Jesus had been out in the sun too long when He told them the Spirit of God was going to now dwell in them!

God's Presence on the Earth

Up until that time, the presence of God dwelt in the Holy of Holies in the Temple. The disciples knew that only the High Priest was allowed to enter the Holy of Holies, and that only happened once a year when he poured blood on the altar as an atonement for the sins of the people.

All Jews knew that the High Priest never casually entered the Holy of Holies. He had to take many precautions to ensure that he was ritually pure. He even left his family a full week before the holiday and stayed in a chamber in the Temple. On the day that he entered the Holy of Holies, he wore a robe that had pomegranates and gold bells sewed into its hem. The purpose for the ornaments was so that those who were outside of the Holy of Holies could hear the bells ringing as he ministered before the Lord. As long as they heard the bells, they knew he was still alive. (Ex. 28:33-35.)

They always had a back-up priest. If the High Priest somehow became "defiled" and could not purify himself in time to complete his duties, the second priest would serve in his place. And, if the High Priest died when he entered the Holy of Holies, the number two priest would have to finish the job. I don't know if I would have ever wanted to have the number two job. If anything happened to the first priest, I would be repenting like crazy before I stepped inside the Holy of Holies!

The disciples were also well aware of the time that Aaron's two sons died when fire from heaven fell because they offered an unauthorized fire to God. (Lev. 10:1,2.) They also remembered how Uzzah died when he grabbed hold of the Ark of the Covenant because he thought it might fall off of the cart that was carrying it to its new home in Jerusalem. (2 Sam. 6:6,7.)

They were familiar with what happened when God told Moses to gather all of the Israelites and bring them to the foot of Mt. Sinai so He could speak to them. Moses gave them very specific instructions on how to approach the mountain. They could not "come as they were" but had to sanctify themselves. They had to wear clean clothes and abstain from sexual relations. Once they got to the mountain, they were told not to touch it or they would die.

On the morning they approached Mt. Sinai, thunder and lightning and a thick cloud that covered the mountain greeted them. Smoke billowed from the mountain as though it was on fire and the whole mountain trembled violently. (Ex. 19:9-19.)

Now, if I were one of the Israelites, you wouldn't have to worry about me getting close to the mountain! I would not have wanted to go anywhere near Mt. Sinai and neither did the children of Israel. In fact, they told Moses, *"You tell us what God says, and we will listen. But don't let God speak directly to us. If he does, we will die!"* (Ex. 20:19 NLT).

This is how the disciples understood the presence of God to be. They had a tremendous reverence for that presence. When Jesus told them that God was going to dwell in them, they must have thought, *Oh no! You're going to put God on the inside of us?*

Charged Up With God's Power

The early church also understood the power that came with the presence of God. They knew if God dwelt inside of them, they could do anything He instructed them to do.

To further explain this, let's pretend that I am a service station attendant. But instead of putting gas in cars, I charge batteries. One day my boss says to me, "Joe, we are not going to use jumper cables anymore. We are going to surgically implant five billion volts of electricity inside of you. We're also going to add some plutonium and a little bit of uranium. Tomorrow, when you come into work, all you will need to do is lay your hands on the batteries, and they will be charged!"

My first thought would be, *You're crazy!* I would tell him to get somebody else, because they were not putting that much power on the inside of me.

That's what the disciples understood would happen to them when Jesus told them that the Spirit of God would dwell in them. They knew that God was a fire from the loins up and a fire from the loins down. (Ezek. 8:2.) And Jesus had the audacity to say, "God is going to dwell in you." But that is exactly what happens when we are baptized in the Holy Spirit. We are endued with power from on high, and that same fire of God dwells on the inside of us.

I like to wear cologne. Just imagine if one day I filled a bathtub with cologne and immersed myself in it. You could say I baptized myself in cologne. The result of my baptism would be that long before I walked through the doors of a church to minister, people would smell me!

We've all been around men and women who wear too much cologne or perfume. When you got close to them, they didn't have to tell you what they were wearing—you just knew it was too much! Even when they left the room, their smell still lingered. Have you ever hugged somebody who had on too much perfume? You may have only embraced for a moment, but that smell got on your clothes and you smelled just like that person!

We are baptized in the Holy Spirit, and we should radiate the power of God everywhere we go. People ought to be able to "smell" the Holy Spirit on us even before we even say a word. They should say, "There is something different about you." It's not because you look good and your hair is in place but because of the presence that you carry in you.

John 7:38 says, *"He that believeth on me, as the scripture hath said, out of his belly shall flow rivers of living water."* I have often sung the song that goes, "I've got a river a life flowing out of me…." I have even preached on that song many times. One day I realized that it wasn't scriptural. The Lord reminded me that I don't have one river flowing out of me but many *rivers* (plural) of living water flowing out of me.

The End-Time Church

If I have many rivers flowing out of me, I better know all the different ways they can flow. That way I will be open to every way that God wants to move through me. In these last days God wants the body of Christ to duplicate everything that Jesus did when He walked on the earth — whether it's raising the dead, cleansing the lepers, or healing the sick.

Jesus had the Spirit of God without measure. Because of that, there was a continual operation of the gifts of healings and working of miracles in His ministry. The fact that Jesus had the Spirit without measure indicates that we have it "with" measure. Whatever measure I have, I need to be ready to operate in it. When the Holy Spirit took up residence in me, I received more power than any atomic weapon we have on the earth. Now I need to learn how to operate in that power so it can transform lives.

We are coming to a time where it will be common to see people raised from the dead. Instead of this type of miracle being performed through the hands of one of the five-fold ministry gifts, ordinary people who are willing to be obedient to the voice of God will be the vessels that God uses.

The end-time outpouring of the Spirit of God is for one reason. God doesn't want anybody to miss the Rapture. But what kind of witness is the end-time church if our lives aren't any different than the unsaved? If we are just as sick, stressed out, and in debt over our eyeballs, why would the unsaved come running to us when things begin to get wild?

In the 2002 Winter Bible Seminar, Dr. Kenneth E. Hagin prophesied that the year 2005 would be a year of judgment. There are going to be a lot of things happening in 2005 that will shake people to the core.

It will also be a time for multitudes of unsaved folks to give their lives to God. After the terrorist attack on the World Trade Center, many news anchors reported that there was a large increase in church attendance across the nation. What do people do when they are afraid? They turn to God, and we need to be ready. By that, I mean everybody, and not just the five-fold ministry gifts.

You need to be able to lead your neighbors to the Lord and get them filled with the Holy Spirit. You also need to be able to lay hands on the sick and see them recover.

This is only going to happen when you are so full of the power of the Holy Spirit that, like Peter, people will fall on their knees to accept the Lord when your shadow falls on them. (Acts 5:15.) God is no respecter of persons. If signs and wonders could be performed through the hands of the early church, the same can happen with you.

Chapter Two

Hearing His Voice

*T*o operate in the gifts of the Spirit, you have to be able to hear the voice of God. How can you receive a word of knowledge and know if God wants you to pray for somebody if you can't hear His voice? Many Christians want God to speak to them in a loud, booming voice. They think they will know for sure it's God if He talks loudly. However, He usually does not speak to His children this way. In fact, it's only recorded three times in the New Testament that God spoke audibly.

When Jesus was baptized in water, the heavens opened and a voice from heaven said, *"...This is my beloved Son, in whom I am well pleased"* (Matt. 3:17). Then, on the Mount of Transfiguration, a voice from a cloud said, *"...This is my beloved Son: hear him"* (Luke 9:35). And finally, we see in the book of John that before Jesus went to Jerusalem, He struggled with completing His mission on earth and earnestly prayed that God would glorify His name. A voice from heaven was heard saying, *"...I have both glorified it, and will glorify it again"* (John 12:28).

After Jesus' ascension into heaven, the church under-
went tremendous persecution. One young Jew who was
particularly zealous in imprisoning Christians was Saul.
But on a trip to the city of Damascus, he had an encounter
with Jesus. A bright light flashed all around him, and a
voice from heaven said, *"Saul, Saul, why persecutest thou me?"*
(Acts 9:4). Not knowing who was questioning him, he
asked, "Who are you?" *"I am Jesus whom thou persecutest: it is
hard for thee to kick against the pricks...Arise, and go into the city,
and it shall be told thee what thou must do"* (vv. 5,6).

We can see that God rarely spoke audibly in the Bible.
We should not seek after audible voices. The Holy Spirit
manifests Himself today through an inward witness. That is
what we should expect. Some of the most awesome manifestations of the Holy Spirit that happened in my ministry
were ones where I was hardly aware of what was going on.

One time during a service, the Lord told me He
wanted to heal somebody's sneeze. I almost missed it
because God didn't shout, "I WANT TO DO SOMETHING IN
THIS SERVICE." This word of knowledge came as a passing
thought. He spoke in a quiet, calm voice—so quiet that it
was easy to miss.

The devil will push you and make you feel compelled to
do something right away. The Holy Spirit never pushes.
He is a perfect gentleman. That is why it's easy to grieve
the Holy Spirit. He respects your free will and will never
"make" you do anything.

The Still, Small Voice

In 1 Kings 18 we have the account of Elijah taking on 450 prophets of Baal at Mount Carmel. Both the prophets of Baal and Elijah built altars. After laying their sacrifices on the altar, the 450 prophets called on Baal to send fire down from heaven and consume their sacrifice. Nothing happened. They cried out to their god all day, but the sacrifice remained untouched.

When it was Elijah's turn, he wanted to make things harder for God. He had the people pour water on the altar three times. Immediately after he called on the name of Jehovah, the fire of God fell and consumed the sacrifice and licked up the water in the trenches. Elijah then commanded the prophets to be seized and killed.

Things were looking pretty good for our man of faith and power until Jezebel, wife of King Ahab, heard what happened. She sent word to the fearless man of God that he was as good as dead. Instead of standing up to the wicked queen, Elijah tucked his tail between his legs and took off running like a scared dog. He eventually reached Mount Horeb, the mountain of God, and spent the night in a cave.

How many times have you encountered some adversity in your life, and instead of getting quiet to hear from God to find out what you should do, you take off running like Elijah? Can you image how puzzled God was? He had just

displayed His power in a mighty way and a short time later Elijah is on the run from a wicked woman.

When God was finally able to get Elijah's attention, He told him to stand at the front of the cave and the Lord would pass by. Elijah felt an earthquake and strong winds. He saw a fire, but God wasn't in any of that. Finally, he heard a still, small voice. The *New International Version* translates it as a "gentle whisper." God simply said, *"What are you doing here, Elijah?"* (1 Kings 19:13 NIV).

Elijah was having a pity party and began to whine to God. *"I have been very jealous for the Lord God of hosts: because the children of Israel have forsaken thy covenant, thrown down thine altars, and slain thy prophets with the sword; and I, even I only, am left; and they seek my life, to take it away"* (1 Kings 19:14). God was neither moved nor impressed by Elijah's tears. He simply told Elijah to get back to doing what he had been instructed to do in the first place.

Then in verse 18, Elijah received a word of knowledge. *"Yet I have left me seven thousand in Israel, all the knees which have not bowed unto Baal, and every mouth which hath not kissed him."* He was not expecting a word of knowledge, but God was finally able to talk with him when he quieted himself down.

Having Ears To Hear

God spoke to Elijah in a still, small voice, and He will do the same with you. If Elijah, who lived under the old dispensation, heard God's voice this way, how much more will today's Christians be able to hear the voice of God with the Holy Spirit living inside of them?

Elijah almost missed it because God's voice was so quiet. The greatest miracles that have happened in my ministry weren't when bursts of lightning pealed outside of the church as I was swinging from the chandeliers! The neatest miracles have occurred when I almost missed it. I'm a wild man and am usually really loud when I minister. I jump on chairs and get in people's faces if I think they are not listening. A lot of times it's after the service is over and my flesh has settled down that I hear what God wants to do.

Once when I ministered in Florida, I thought the service was finished. I had already turned the meeting back to the pastor. That's when I finally got quiet and heard the Lord say, "I want to heal somebody's fingernails."

I thought, *Fingernails? I'm not calling that out; that's too strange.* Even though I wanted to sit down and let the pastor close the service, I turned around and said, "Who has trouble with your fingernails?" A lady came to the altar and told me that because she had been a premature baby, her fingernails had never fully developed. I laid hands on her, and the Lord healed her.

Sometimes we think that if there is going to be an awesome move of the Spirit of God, people have to shake.

Although people have been known to vibrate under the power of God, it's not a prerequisite for God to heal somebody. Many times when God speaks, it's not that spectacular, although the end result of what He says is often very spectacular.

The End-Time Move of God

We think we know how God will do things during a service. But in these last days, we are going to have to throw out our preconceived ideas. I believe there will come a day that instead of young children only being recipients of God's power, they will say to their pastor, "I have a word." We are going to see the power of God flow through youngsters as they lay hands on people nobody thought could get healed, and we are going to see the miraculous happen.

I asked the Lord one time, "What is it going be like before You return? I want to know."

"If I told you," He said, "you would not believe it."

"Lord, I can believe for some pretty wild things," I said. "I can believe that thousands of people can get saved in one service. I can believe that every person with Down Syndrome will be set free. I can believe that every blind person who comes to a service will receive his or her sight."

You might have thought that stuff like this would only happen through missionaries in places like Peru or Afghanistan. No, this is for everybody, especially for Christians in the United States. America has sowed the Gospel around the world for the past 200 years. It's time for us to reap the supernatural manifestations that have been happening in foreign countries for hundreds of years.

Be Quiet Once in a While

Most everybody has had guests stay with them at one time or another. Wouldn't it be rude if you never allowed your guests to speak? Every time they got around you, you started to talk and wouldn't let them say one word. They would try to say something, but you kept cutting them off.

This very thing happens with the Holy Spirit. He dwells on the inside of us and wants to talk to us every day. Many times, however, we don't give Him the opportunity to say a word.

One of the things that will allow the Holy Spirit to manifest Himself is having an intimate relationship with Him. No relationship is one-sided. In a good relationship, both people communicate. We have to learn how to have a dialogue with the Holy Spirit instead of constantly telling Him all of our needs and concerns.

You can talk to the Holy Spirit wherever you are. You can be in the middle of a big city with sirens blaring and horns honking, or you can be hiking in the middle of nowhere. The Holy Spirit will speak to you in both places. You don't have to wait until you are in church to have a conversation with Him either. But what's more important than your talking to Him, is that you are able to hear what He is saying back to you.

Led by the Holy Spirit

The key to being ready for the Holy Spirit to manifest Himself is to be led by the Spirit of God. Romans 8:14 says, *"For as many as are led by the Spirit of God, they are the sons of God."* I want to show you the difference between an ordinary leading and a manifestation of the Holy Spirit.

Many years ago, I had a sales job where I worked with some guys who were professional sinners. They liked to sin and were very good at it! One day as I was putting money into a Coke machine, some coins fell out of the changer holder onto the floor. As I reached down to pick up the change, the Holy Spirit nudged my heart; and I knew I was supposed to leave the money on the floor.

Shortly after I got back to my desk, my coworker, James, came into the office. He said, "I can't believe it! The guy who works for the Coca-Cola Company found some change on the floor. Now he's happy because he gives the money he finds to a children's home."

"You know that money he found on the ground?" I said, "I left it there because the Lord told me to."

"You're nuts!" he said.

"Yeah, I know," I said. "But that's all right."

Two weeks later, the sales staff went out to lunch at a local restaurant. As I was walking back toward the restroom the Holy Spirit suddenly manifested. I didn't shake. I didn't quiver. I didn't see any lightning. I was just walking toward the restroom when I heard the Lord clearly say, "James has a call on his life."

I thought, *A call on his life? The devil called this guy.* I said, "Lord, You got the wrong guy!" But because I knew I had heard from God, I also knew I would have to say something to him. When we were leaving the restaurant, I said, "James, the Lord told me you have a call on your life."

He looked at me for a long time without saying a word. Finally, he said, "I sure do. When I was 16, I was going to be a preacher. I've been running from God my whole life."

If you will learn to obey the Holy Spirit in the small leadings (like leaving the change on the floor by the Coke machine), then you will put yourself in a position to receive a manifestation of the Holy Spirit. I received a word of knowledge when the Lord told me that James was called to

the ministry. The two go hand-in-hand. If you will never obey the inward witness, you will never receive a manifestation of the Spirit.

Stay Filled With the Holy Spirit

How do we put ourselves in a position to hear the Holy Spirit's voice? Ephesians 5:17-18 says, *"Wherefore be ye not unwise, but understanding what the will of the Lord is. And be not drunk with wine, wherein is excess; but be filled with the Spirit."*

Although you were baptized in the Holy Spirit and speak in tongues, you need to be continually filled with the Holy Spirit. The fuller you are, the easier it will be for the Holy Spirit to manifest Himself through you. When you spend time in the Word—reading and studying it—as well as praying in the Spirit, you are being "refilled" with the Holy Spirit.

You can tell when your Holy Spirit level is low. Everything bothers you. Your pastor irritates you. Instead of things working out for you, you are constantly hitting brick walls. But as soon as you get back in church and spend time with the Lord, you can actually feel the difference on the inside of you.

If you filled a glass with water until it was about three-fourths full, you could swirl the water around in the glass without spilling any of it. However, if you fill the glass to the very top, you only have to bump the glass and the water will spill out. That's what happens when you are full of the Holy Spirit. All the Holy Spirit has to do is nudge you a little, and He will pour out.

When Paul told the church at Ephesus to be full of the Holy Spirit, he was telling them to be ready for the Holy Spirit to manifest Himself through them. If we will learn to obey the still, small voice, then we will be ready when the Holy Spirit wants to manifest Himself through us in a big way.

Chapter Three

Kingdom Living

*A*fter the day of Pentecost, the early church gave themselves to constant study of the Word and prayer. The church grew so fast that in a short period of time the disciples were not able to teach the Word anymore. Instead, they were consumed with feeding the people. It quickly became apparent that some things had to change. They called the believers together and said,

> *It is not reason that we should leave the word of God, and serve tables. Wherefore, brethren, look ye out among you seven men of honest report, full of the Holy Ghost and wisdom, whom we may appoint over this business. But we will give ourselves continually to prayer, and to the ministry of the word.*
>
> ACTS 6:2-4

The qualifications the apostles looked for in choosing men who would take their place to wait on tables were to be full of faith and full of the Holy Spirit. They did not

care if the person had ever been a waiter before; they wanted to know how many miracles he had performed.

I wonder how long it would take to fill a position like this today. Can you imagine your pastor posting this advertisement in the church bulletin?

> *Waiter Wanted. Job duties include waiting tables and clean up afterwards. Qualifications: Must be full of faith and power and have documented evidence of performing great wonders and miracles in the last six months.*

What may even be more amazing is that they found, not one, but seven men who met these qualifications. (v. 5.) The Scripture doesn't say anything about a lengthy search. They looked among the people and quickly found these men. It seems like we might be hard pressed to find one person who could fill that position today.

Look what happened when the apostles put these men in charge of doing the "menial" tasks of the early church. *"And the word of God increased; and the number of the disciples multiplied in Jerusalem greatly..."* (v. 7).

Christians today seem to be either full of faith or full of the Holy Spirit. They tend to be on one side or the other. However, when you are full of both, things start happening. This was evidenced in Stephen's life. We see in the book of Acts that he performed great wonders and miracles. (v. 8.)

Isn't it interesting that they had to qualify his miracles? Not only did he do miracles, but he also did "great" wonders. Most of us would be satisfied with miracles. They differentiated between the miraculous and the super miraculous.

I believe we are in store for this today. We have had the uncompromised Word preached for the past 25 years and have recently been experiencing the move of the Spirit. Now that the two have combined, the church is full of faith *and* full of the Holy Spirit. It's time for the end-time church to start demonstrating the works of Jesus the same way the early church did.

Demonstrating the Kingdom

In Jesus' ministry, somebody got healed or delivered all the time. In fact, the miracles that are recorded in the four Gospels are only a fraction of what He did. John 21:25 says that if all of the miracles were written down, the world would not have room enough to store all of the books.

If healings and miracles were common when Jesus was on the earth, how could the apostles' and disciples' ministries be anything less? The same should hold true for us as well. We need to be like Jesus in every way and demonstrate His power, love, and mercy to those around us.

Another disciple that made headline news in the early church was Philip. Even though Philip's primary "ministry" was waiting tables in Jerusalem, he also had a traveling ministry on the side.

When he traveled to the region of Samaria and preached Christ to the people, they listened to what he had to say because of the miracles that were performed through him.

> *And the people with one accord gave heed unto those things which Philip spake, hearing and seeing the miracles which he did. For unclean spirits, crying with loud voice, came out of many that were possessed with them: and many taken with palsies, and that were lame, were healed.*
>
> ACTS 8:6,7

Philip had one message: The kingdom of God is near because of the name of Jesus. (Acts 8:12.) When he preached this, people were healed and evil spirits left. He understood that some people wouldn't "bite" until they saw the evidence.

Philip knew what the kingdom was. It was not religion or tradition. It is Almighty God residing in men and women. Paul said, *"We have this treasure in earthen vessels, that the excellency of the power may be of God, and not of us"* (2 Cor. 4:7).

Philip knew that it was the power of God working through Him that caused the miraculous to happen. He understood the authority and power that dwelt inside of him.

When Jesus commissioned the seventy disciples to preach in nearby villages and lay hands on the sick, He told them to tell whomever would listen that the kingdom of God has come nigh unto them. (Luke 10:9.)

When people understand that the kingdom of God is near, they will experience liberty in ways they have never known before. The kingdom of God eradicates disease, fear, and all impossibilities.

Even though Christians today are filled with the Holy Spirit and walk in faith, they are not kingdom-minded. If they were, we would see the same miracles, signs, and wonders performed today that the early church experienced.

Many believers today don't have the same reverence for the name of Jesus that the early church had. Even though we have been taught faith and how to move in the Holy Spirit, most people don't have confidence in the name of Jesus.

When the early church magnified and exalted Jesus' name, they expected and saw miracles happen. We don't see that today.

The apostles were often commanded to stop preaching in the name of Jesus. The high priest said to them in Acts 5:28, *"Did not we straitly command you that ye should not teach in*

this name?" I have never had anybody command me to stop preaching in the name of Jesus, have you?

A More Excellent Name

The early church understood the power that came with the name of Jesus. They knew if they preached in His name, heaven would back them up. That is why they made such an impact in Jerusalem.

When you talk about that name, you have the power that goes with it. You do not have to work to get it; it's just there. Philip and Stephen were just like you and me. They were regular guys who loved the Lord. What set them apart from others was the Word of God, the Holy Spirit, and the name of Jesus.

When the angel Gabriel appeared to Mary, he told her that she was to name her son Jesus. (Luke 1:31.) Jesus was a common name at that time. Some popular baby names today include Jacob, Matthew, Michael, and Joshua. If Jesus were born today, He could have been given any one of these names. What is the difference between Jesus' name and the other Jesuses who were born at that time?

We see in the following verses that Jesus received His name by conquest and by inheritance.

...when he had by himself purged our sins, sat down on the right hand of the Majesty on high: Being made so much

better than the angels, as he hath by inheritance obtained a more excellent name than they.

HEBREWS 1:3,4

After Jesus died on the Cross, He descended into hell and *"...spoiled principalities and powers, he made a shew of them openly, triumphing over them in it"* (Col. 2:15). After He triumphed over the devil and took back the keys of hell and the grave, He proclaimed victory and burst out of the pit of hell.

Devils do not like to hear the name of Jesus. It brings back too many bad memories. All of hell clearly remembers when Jesus was raised from the dead. That is the day when Satan and all of his hordes were put under Jesus' feet.

Demons are glad when Christians do not understand the authority that that name commands. When you don't use the name of Jesus, you are giving them permission to continue wreaking havoc in your life.

Because of Jesus' obedience, even unto death, God exalted Him and gave Him a name above every name. (Phil. 2:9,10.) Jesus received the stamp of the resurrection when He came up out of the pit.

When Lazarus died, Jesus told his sister, "I am the resurrection." (John 11:25.) When you mention His name, you should think about the resurrection power.

One time I prayed for a young girl who had brain cancer. I later learned that the doctors had only given her two weeks to live. Her parents brought her down to the altar for prayer, and I boldly proclaimed in the name of Jesus that she was healed. They looked at me as though I were crazy. I said a second time, "You are healed in the name of Jesus, the name that is above every name. Cancer is below the name of Jesus."

When I was ministering to her, I was not thinking about my qualifications or how long I had been in the ministry. I was only thinking about the power behind Jesus' name and how nothing on earth was equal to it. A week later when the girl went to the doctor, he said the cancer was gone!

I was ministering in Bonn, Germany, when a woman who looked gravely ill stood before me in the healing line. I laid my hands on her and commanded her to be healed in the name of Jesus. It wasn't long before I received a testimony that she had been healed of full blown aids!

Experiencing the Resurrection

We need to experience the resurrection power that was obtained for us. Unfortunately, people limit that power. To God there isn't any difference between healing a cold or healing cancer. That power can do more than heal a

headache; it can recreate a heart, restore a missing limb, and raise the dead.

An example of what that power can do is found in the Old Testament. When Elijah asked Elisha what he wanted before he was taken away, Elisha replied, *"I pray thee, let a double portion of thy spirit be upon me"* (2 Kings 2:9.) What is interesting is that Elisha's final miracle happened after he had died.

Not long after Elisha had been buried, some Israelites were burying a man when suddenly they saw a band of Moabite raiders. Fearing for their lives, they quickly threw the man in Elisha's tomb and then hid from their enemies.

When the dead man's body touched Elisha's bones, he came to life and stood on his feet. (2 Kings 13:20,21.) That is how strong the anointing of God is!

The Power of the Name

We are Word people, but we have forgotten what it takes for the miraculous to occur. Jesus of Nazareth. God made it simple and uncomplicated for us. It's all in the name of Jesus. Anybody can call on that name. Whether you are 2 or 80, you can call on that name and see miracles.

Before Jesus ascended to heaven in Mark 16, He appeared to two of the disciples who *"...went and told it unto the residue: neither believed they them"* (v. 13). Scripture calls

them "the residue," because they didn't believe the people who had seen Jesus after He was raised from the dead.

When Jesus appeared to the eleven, He rebuked them for their lack of faith. He did not dwell on the disciples' unbelief. He immediately commissioned them to *"Go…"* in verse 15. This is what the church is all about—going out and preaching the kingdom of God.

He immediately brought to their attention that He now has superiority over the god of this world when He said, "In My Name you will drive out devils." (v. 17.) He wanted them to understand the dominance they now have over the devil. He told them that the power is in His name—not in slick preaching, tradition, or Bible school—but in the name of Jesus.

After Jesus commissioned them to go, they *"…went forth, and preached every where, the Lord working with them and confirming the word with signs following"* (Mark 16:20). They magnified the name of Jesus and preached the kingdom of God. If you want to see more signs and wonders in your life, then follow the example of the early church by magnifying the name of Jesus.

One time Reverend R.W. Schambach was ministering in India. He was irritated that he wasn't seeing the results that he wanted. He prayed, "Lord, I didn't come all this way not to have any miracles."

At the next service, he saw a blind man. He walked up to him and said, "In the name of Jesus, eyes be opened." The man's eyes were instantly opened. He then went to the man in a wheelchair and said, "In the name of Jesus, rise up and walk." The man stood up and began to walk.

He saw a man lying on a cot and said, "In the name of Buddha, rise up and walk." Nothing happened. "In the name of Mohammed, rise up and walk." Nothing happened. "In the name of Reverend Moon, rise up and walk." Nothing happened.

Finally he said, "In the name of Jesus Christ of Nazareth, rise up and walk." That man immediately jumped off the cot!

All authority lies in that name. Everything that has a name has to bow to the name of Jesus. (Eph. 1:21.) That is the name that sets people free. When we magnify and speak in that name, we will see the miraculous happen.

Commanding Devils To Leave

One time I was preaching in the Ukraine in an old civic center. The building was so dilapidated that it looked like it would fall down at any moment. The pastor of the church there had only been saved for two years.

After the Word had gone forth, we were laying hands
on the sick. We were having a wonderful time in the Lord
ministering to the sick when a woman began to scream.

When we got to her, she was levitating. Three or four of
the ushers were trying to hold her down. The pastor said,
"Oh, my God. She's floating!" The first thing that came to
my mind was, *How dare you interrupt what God is doing?*

I said to the woman, "Look at me right now." Her eyes
were darting all over. She would not look me in the eyes. I
grabbed her by the shirt and said, "Look at me, in Jesus'
name!" When she looked at me, I said, "Come out of her."

I did not scream; I commanded the devil to leave in a
normal tone. You don't have to scream at the devil. You
can whisper the name of Jesus, and he has to obey you.
The woman immediately settled down and quit being a
hovercraft. Peace came over her face. Those demons had
no choice but to bow at the name.

Another time I was ministering in Pittsburgh,
Pennsylvania. We were having a wonderful time laying
hands on the people. A little girl had fallen out under the
power. She later told her pastor that Jesus appeared to her
and gave her a tour of heaven.

A woman who had become blind because of diabetes
received her sight. A young girl had been healed of

leukemia. When she went to the doctor the next day, he said the cancer had disappeared. That name doesn't just make you recover; it also eradicates disease and death.

As we were ministering, the ushers came up to me and whispered, "Brother Joe. There's a crazy lady in the back of the church!" When I reached the woman, she was shaking and growling, "I hate the pastor's wife! I hate the pastor's mother!" I'm thinking, *Why, you little devil. How dare you interrupt this service!*

When she saw me, she growled, "I hate you! I'm going to kill you! I'm going to kill your family!" Then she said with a wicked smile, "You can't cast me out!"

"Oh, yeah?" I said. "Look at me right now." When she looked at me, I said, "Come out of her in Jesus' name." She hit the floor like a sack of potatoes.

This woman was bold. If a woman can get so full of the devil that she can boldly threaten to kill me, you can be filled with the Holy Spirit to the point where you boldly cast devils out of oppressed people.

The devil can be that bold because Christians cower in fear when he manifests himself. Even though Jesus defeated Satan and all of his cohorts, many Christians don't act like it.

Knowing What You Have

One time I was given tickets to the U.S. Open. I went with a friend, and we sat in the hot sun for three days watching the matches. I love sports and had an awesome time. On the last day, I saw the guy who gave me the tickets.

He said, "Have you been in the clubhouse and had a chance to talk to any of the players?"

"No, I'm out here in the heat, in these tee boxes," I said. "I'm having a good time and am thrilled to be here."

"Well, duh," he said. "Look at your badges. You don't have to stay out in the heat. You can go in the clubhouse and get anything you want!"

There were three types of badges. One badge had *Grounds* written on it. Another *Clubhouse,* and the third had *All* written on it. I did not know what my badge meant, so I spent most of the time in the heat. With the badge that I had on, I could not only go in the clubhouse or in the locker rooms and meet the players, I could also eat all of the food they were serving the VIPs.

That's the way it is with many Christians. We have a badge called the name of Jesus, and we have access to the throne of God. We can go to the throne and take whatever we need.

We have been sitting in the heat saying, "Wow, this is a great revival. I wish I could flow in the Holy Spirit like that. I wish I could see miracles." You don't know that the badge you are wearing gives you access to the power of God.

Jesus gave us His authority in His name. One time as I was praying, the Lord said, "Why are you talking to Me about this? You have authority; use it."

We often wait for Jesus to do something, but He is waiting on us. As we change our mindset from a defeated Christian to living a resurrection lifestyle, we will boldly use the name of Jesus. Jesus paid the price and defeated the devil. Now, we just have to walk in what He did.

Chapter Four

Bold as a Lion

*T*he Apostle Peter's first letter was a message of encouragement, instruction, and admonition to the Christians who were scattered throughout Asia Minor. Even though he was part of Jesus' inner circle and was a pillar in the early church, he opens his letter by calling himself a servant.

"Simon Peter, a servant and an apostle of Jesus Christ..." (2 Peter 1:1). This shows you that it does not matter how long you have been a Christian or how mightily the Lord uses you, you are always a servant.

The purpose for the gifts of the Spirit is to minister to the needs of people. They were never meant to make you look more "spiritual" or to draw attention to yourself. Neither were they meant to only flow to you. Jesus intended that you would be an unselfish vessel He could use in the manifestation of the gifts of the Spirit. They are ministry tools to break the bondage of the devil over people's lives.

In speaking of the coming Christ, John the Baptist said, *"He must increase, but I must decrease"* (John 3:30). As you begin to step out in the gifts of the Spirit, you must remember that you have to take a backseat so that God can do what He wants to do.

Everybody should be operating in the gifts of the Spirit. If all Christians would do so, they would not be so awed by people who move in the Spirit. Moving in the gifts should be as ordinary as walking down the street.

If you are not sure how to get from where you are to confidently operating in the gifts of the Spirit, you can begin with prayer.

Praying for Boldness

While it is not scriptural to pray for faith, you can ask God for boldness. Very soon after the early church had received the Baptism of the Holy Spirit, we see them petition God for it.

Peter and John had been jailed overnight because the lame man at the Gate Beautiful had been healed. After their release, they went to their fellow Christians and told them how the chief priests and elders had threatened them.

When the believers heard the report, they did not become fearful and wonder what their future would hold.

Nor did they back off from what Jesus had commissioned them to do. Instead, the entire company prayed for boldness.

> *And now, Lord, behold their threatenings: and grant unto thy servants, that with all boldness they may speak thy word, By stretching forth thine hand to heal; and that signs and wonders may be done by the name of thy holy child Jesus. And when they had prayed, the place was shaken where they were assembled together; and they were all filled with the Holy Ghost, and they spake the word of God with boldness.*

ACTS 4:29-31

It did not bother Peter or John that they had been thrown in jail. They did not feel that their reputations were ruined in the Jewish community because of this run-in with the high priests. Their only concern was that they would not back away from what they had been called to do. They wanted to continue preaching the Word with boldness.

After they had prayed, the place was shaken and they were filled with the Holy Spirit. What is interesting here is that they were initially filled with the Holy Spirit in the second chapter of Acts. Then, in chapter four, they were filled again.

I think that many Christians believe that the Baptism of the Holy Spirit is a one-shot deal, but that is not true. As you give out, you need to be filled back up again. You can

guarantee that you will always stay full of the Holy Spirit by praying in tongues (Jude 20) and by never neglecting your fellowship time with the Lord.

What happened after the disciples prayed? They went back out on the streets and continued preaching the Word. The Scripture says that *"...with great power gave the apostles witness of the resurrection of the Lord Jesus: and great grace was upon them all"* (Acts 4:33). They refused to let anything—even the threat of jail—keep them from proclaiming the Word.

Knowing Your Rights

Knowing your rights also makes you bold. Let's say that a clerk at a gas station convenience store is shot and killed. The police happen to be pulling into the parking lot as the crime is taking place.

In the confusion of the moment, the police arrest an innocent bystander instead of the man who shot the clerk. Even though the man tries to protest, the police haul him off to jail. The killer is able to slip out the door, laughing at the mistake that was made.

I guarantee you that the man who was taken to jail would be bold about his rights. He would demand to make a phone call to get in touch with a lawyer, so they could begin the task of proving his innocence. It is an injustice

when an innocent person is sent to prison for a crime that he or she did not commit.

It is just as much of an injustice when you suffer with sickness or lack. Jesus paid the penalty for our sins, sicknesses, and poverty on the Cross.

I'm sure the family of a wrongly accused person rallies around the individual. In the same way, when somebody becomes sick or is oppressed by the devil, we need to rally around that individual and demand that the devil take his hands off of the person.

You can be bold in your faith when you know what God has promised you in His Word. But *you* have to be the one who boldly demands your rights. Too often, Christians run to their pastor or call a ministry for prayer instead of standing up for their rights.

They do not realize that they can take authority over the situation in the name of Jesus. You would speak up in the natural if somebody tried to arrest you without a cause. Why do you allow the devil to bring sickness or adversity without objecting?

good example

A Defeated Foe

Let's say that as you were leaving a grocery store, the security officer followed you to your car and accused you of stealing the bags of groceries you were carrying. You

wouldn't even need to argue with him. All you would have to do is show him your receipt to prove that you paid for everything.

We need to do that same thing with the devil. We have to let him know that our receipt has been signed for by the blood of Jesus and then tell him to back off!

Most people would be indignant if a security officer tried to accuse them of stealing when they didn't. God is the same way. He becomes indignant when His children do not walk in what has been provided for them. He is shaking His head, thinking, *Don't you know the price I paid so you could be set free? Don't you know the devil is defeated?*

Many Christians act as though the devil is more powerful than God. He is nothing more than a wimp with a big mouth. Satan is all talk with no power to back up his actions. The only power he has is what you give him. Remember he walks around *as* a lion seeking whom he may devour. (1 Peter 5:8.)

If you could see into the spirit realm, you would see that he is like an emaciated pit bull that had his teeth pulled. Jesus stripped him of his power and authority when He descended into hell. Unfortunately, too many people give heed to what the devil whispers in their ears.

When John Osteen was alive, he told the story about a friend of his who had a vision of the devil. The man

suddenly found himself in a dark valley and felt as though he was in the region of the damned.

He looked up and saw the devil walking toward him, and fear gripped his heart. As the devil got closer, Jesus appeared in front of the man, facing the devil. Jesus then backed inside of the man's body. When Satan reached the two of them, Jesus said through the man, "Bow."

This is a great reminder of who we have dwelling on the inside of us. When we use our authority and command the devil to stop, it's not as though we are speaking; Jesus is. The devil does not have any choice but to submit to that name.

After the 70 returned from preaching the kingdom of God to people in towns and villages throughout Israel, Jesus said, *"I beheld Satan as lightning fall from heaven"* (Luke 10:18).

God did not have a pushing match in heaven trying to get the devil to leave. God cast Satan out of heaven so fast that he didn't know what hit him.

Standing Up to a Wicked King

Signs and wonders can happen in your life in the same way that it did in the early church if you would boldly stand on the Word. One of the definitions of the word *bold* in the *Random House Unabridged Dictionary* means "to dare."

Not that you are afraid to do something, but that you boldly dare to do something.

Great example of boldness

When Shadrach, Meshach, and Abednego were commanded to worship the golden image that King Nebuchadnezzar had made, they refused. The King had the three young men brought before him and threatened to have them thrown into a fiery furnace if they refused to worship the golden image. He mockingly said to them, *"...and who is that God that shall deliver you out of my hands?"* (Daniel 3:15).

The young men did not flinch. They knew where their trust was. Here is how they replied to the king's threats:

> *O Nebuchadnezzar, we are not careful to answer thee in this matter. If it be so, our God whom we serve is able to deliver us from the burning fiery furnace, and he will deliver us out of thine hand, O king. But if not, be it known unto thee, O king, that we will not serve thy gods, nor worship the golden image which thou hast set up.*
>
> DANIEL 3:16-18

Nebuchadnezzar was not used to people standing up to him. Usually they complied with everything he said. He was furious when they talked to him this way. How dare they? Didn't they know who he was?

To make matters worse, they provoked him with their answer. They did not say, "If God doesn't deliver us, we will fry." No, they said, "If you have the guts to throw us in

the fire, our God is able to deliver us. If you don't have enough guts to execute us, we still won't worship your god." In essence, they dared him to go ahead and do what he said!

These young men scared Nebuchadnezzar. You can tell from his actions that he was afraid that God would help them out. He did not use regular soldiers to deliver them to the furnace.

He had the strongest men in his army bind them and throw them in the furnace. Then he had the fire stoked up seven times hotter, just in case. After taking these measures, he felt confident that there was no way they could survive.

Like Nebuchadnezzar, the devil does not expect people to stand up to him. Most people, and even Christians, back off when he rears his ugly head. It shocks him when somebody uses his or her authority against him. Most Christians do not talk to him as though he is under their feet. They give him far more reverence than he deserves.

How did Shadrach, Meshach, and Abednego fare? Did their boldness pay off?

Shadrach, Meshach, and Abednego, fell down bound into the midst of the burning fiery furnace. Then Nebuchadnezzar the king was astonished, and rose up in haste, and spake, and said unto his counsellors, Did not we cast three men bound into the midst of the fire? They

*answered and said unto the king, True, O king. He
answered and said, Lo, I see four men loose, walking in the
midst of the fire, and they have no hurt; and the form of the
fourth is like the Son of God.*

DANIEL 3:23-25

We need to remember these three Hebrews the next
time we feel like we are caught between a rock and a hard
place. The lesson to learn is, if you do not bow, you will not
burn. If you will not compromise, God will show up every
time. If you will be bold, the Holy Spirit will manifest. God
will go over a million people and move heaven and earth if
you will believe His Word.

Look at what happened because of their boldness. Only
moments before, Nebuchadnezzar said, "Who is your God
that He can save you from my hands?" Now he called to
the young men *"...servants of the Most High God"* (v. 26). He
quickly had a change of heart and acknowledged who God
was. He went on to say,

*Blessed be the God of Shadrach, Meshach, and Abednego,
who hath sent his angel, and delivered his servants that
trusted in him, and have changed the king's word, and
yielded their bodies, that they might not serve nor worship
any god, except their own God. Therefore I make a decree,
That every people, nation, and language, which speak any
thing amiss against the God of Shadrach, Meshach, and
Abednego, shall be cut in pieces, and their houses shall be*

made a dunghill: because there is no other God that can deliver after this sort.

DANIEL 3:28,29

Not only were they delivered from the furnace, their boldness also delivered their nation. The king decreed that the entire nation should stop worshipping idols and begin worshipping the true God.

Double Dog Dare

If Christians will be bold or daring enough, people would listen to what they say and follow God. Have you ever been dared to do something? My brother is about ten years older than me, and he could be pretty cold-blooded when we were growing up. He was a good guy, but cold-blooded.

When I was a kid, we lived on a lake and water skied all the time. My brother was a great skier. In fact, he did not have to jump into the water to get started. He would sit on the edge of the dock with his water skis on.

After the boat took off, he would "pop off" the dock and land on top of the water. When he wanted to stop skiing, the boat would swing close to the docks and he would whip into the shore. Most of the time, he never really got wet.

I used to watch him and wish that I could pop off. I just didn't have the guts to try it. One day my brother said to me, "I dare you to learn how to pop off."

"I'm only ten," I argued.

He put his face right in mine and said, "I double dog dare you!"

Oh, why did he double dog dare me? I couldn't let a double dog dare go by. Now I *had* to do it—even though I didn't want to! I had a sick feeling in the pit of my stomach as I sat at the end of the dock. I had them take up most of the slack in the rope. There was just enough slack so the boat could have some acceleration before it got to me.

Well, my brother gunned the engine; and before I knew it, all of the slack in the rope was gone. I shot off that dock like a rocket and went skipping across the water face first! It never crossed my mind to let go of the rope. My brother drug me halfway around the lake before he stopped! I was stupid enough to try it again. I drank so much lake water that I was sick the next day.

My brother dared me to do a pop off because he knew how to do it. You don't dare somebody unless you can do it yourself. You see, knowledge makes you very bold.

Bold as a Lion

I have never seen a cowardly lion. They always look like they can rip your head off, even when they are in a cage. They have a look about them that almost dares you to mess with them. It's like they are saying, "Go ahead. I dare you to come near this cage."

I grew up in Louisiana and went to a lot of LSU Tiger football games. The mascot for the college was Mike the tiger. Before football games, they brought the tiger out in a cage and somebody would pull him around the track.

One day we got to the football field early, and I snuck out on the track where the tiger was. He was peacefully lying in his cage, and I thought I would mess with him. I crept up to the cage and was going to poke him with a stick.

I was pretty close when he lifted his head and ROARED! I jumped back so fast I thought my heart flew out of my mouth! I never messed with that tiger again. Never!

Proverbs 28:1 says, *"The wicked flee when no man pursueth, but the righteous are as bold as a lion."* We need to start walking around like lions and show some attitude on our faces. We need to be bold and not scared. When we start acting like this, we will start doing the works of Jesus.

I am naturally bold; but when the gift of special faith comes on me, that boldness is increased 100-fold. One time

I had a word of knowledge about a woman who had been in a car accident. That gift of special faith came on me, and I had a vision of her dancing. I said, "I'm going to point at you, and you're going to throw your hands up and start dancing. Once you do, you will be instantly healed."

It wasn't my faith or her faith that brought about her healing. It was God's faith. She started dancing when I pointed at her and was instantly healed.

I like the boldness that comes on you when the gift of faith manifests. There is a daringness to your faith and what you say. It is a powerful faith where you command the devil to BACK OFF, and he doesn't have any choice but to obey.

Be Bold in Your Faith

The Lord told me one time that if I would be bolder in my Christian walk, He could use me in the gift of special faith more often. When He said this, I was reminded of the different personalities of the apostles. Have you ever noticed which apostle was used the most in the gift of special faith? If you're thinking Peter, you're right.

Peter was the boldest and most radical of all the apostles. He was far from perfect, but he was bold. He was the one who jumped out of the boat and walked on water. (Matt. 14:29.) It was Peter who suggested that they build

three tabernacles on the Mount of Transfiguration. (Mark 9:5.)

He was also known for his crazy actions. Peter cut off the ear of a man in the Garden of Gethsemane. (John 18:10.) He had the attitude, "Man, I'm going for it." On the day of Pentecost, Peter was the one who pointed his finger in the religious leaders' faces, saying, "You crucified the Lord of glory!" (Acts 3:14,15.)

Peter operated in the gift of faith in the book of Acts more than anybody else. It was Peter, not John, who grabbed the lame man's hand by the Gate Beautiful and pulled him to his feet. (Acts 3:7.) Peter commanded Aeneas, a man who had been paralyzed for eight years, to rise from his bed and walk. (Acts 9:32-34.) He also raised a woman from the dead. (Acts 9:36-40.)

We can see from Peter's life that the bolder we are, the more God can use us. It takes boldness to witness to somebody. It also takes boldness to pray for somebody who has cancer. It takes daringness. You cannot be concerned about what people will think. After all, who do you answer to? Them or God?

The reason we do not see more miracles happen today is because most people are more afraid of what people will think about them than they are about God. It shouldn't be that way. If they would spend more time with God, they

would realize that it is His approval that they need and not man's.

I want to encourage you to step out like Peter and just "go for it." Even though Peter was impulsive and did and said things that were not always cool, God was able to use him in the gifts of the Spirit more than the other disciples. Sure he made mistakes, and probably you will too. The important thing is to keep on moving forward in the things of God.

The prophet Micah said, *"Rejoice not against me, O mine enemy: when I fall, I shall arise…"* (Micah 7:8). If you miss it, pick yourself up and keep going. Never, never stop. The next time you just might raise somebody from the dead. Let's go for it in the time that we have left on the earth and put a smile on God's face.

Chapter Five

Get Ready To Be Used!

*I*n explaining spiritual gifts to the church at Corinth, Paul begins, *"Now concerning spiritual gifts, brethren, I would not have you ignorant"* (1 Cor. 12:1). In most Bibles the word *gifts* is italicized. That means it was not in the original Greek. It was added by the translators to give readers better clarity. This verse could be read: *"Now concerning spiritual brethren, I would not have you ignorant."*

You can go through life being ignorant of things. I don't know how to fix the fuel injection in my car. But then again, I don't need to know. I can easily get somebody to fix it for me. I would not know how to repair my refrigerator if it ever needed fixed, but I can get somebody to fix that as well.

While I don't have to know all things, there are some things that I should be well versed in, namely the Word of God, the name of Jesus, and spiritual gifts. Paul told the Corinthian church, "You should not be ignorant." In other words, don't be misinformed about spiritual gifts.

Tools of the Trade

God gave us equipment to demonstrate a resurrection lifestyle. They are the rivers of water that He wants to flow out of us. We call them the manifestations of the Holy Spirit. They are harvesting tools God wants us to use to spread the Gospel. It's important then that we understand how to use them.

If you were a carpenter, you would need to know how different power tools operate. Imagine trying to use a miter saw when you needed to make small, intricately curved cuts. What you need is a jig saw. A miter saw would never get the job done. The same is true with the gifts of the Spirit. To operate effectively, you need to understand how each one works.

That is why Paul wrote his first letter to the Corinthian church. They operated so freely in the Holy Spirit that there was chaos during their services. People wanted to prophesy or give out a word of knowledge or a word of wisdom while the Word was being preached. God likes things to be done decently and in order, and the church services at Corinth definitely needed order.

When I was young, there was a couple in my church who would give out tongues and an interpretation of tongues just about every Sunday. The woman would speak in tongues, and the man always started the interpretation by saying, "The sun will rise in the East and set in the

West...." It never failed. You could count on them to do this every Sunday.

Paul didn't want the church to be ignorant in how to operate in the gifts of the Spirit and neither do I. He told Timothy to *"study to shew thyself approved unto God, a workman that needeth not to be ashamed..."* (2 Tim. 2:15). It's important that we take the time to learn how to operate in the gifts of the Spirit and not be found ashamed in what we do.

Supernatural Manifestations

Unfortunately, the gifts of the Spirit have lain dormant for almost 2,000 years, but we're coming to a time where we are going see them explode on the earth. I believe before Jesus returns, the church will once again walk in the same power and authority that the early church did.

You have heard the saying, "talk is cheap." God wants to do some things that will grab people's attention. For some people, only a supernatural manifestation will enable God to get through to them. They will then realize that He really cares because of what He has done. I was ministering in a prayer line one time when a man walked up to me and said, "I don't even believe this stuff, but I just got healed!" Once people know that God is for them and not against them, they become more open to hear the Gospel.

When Jesus was transfigured, the Scripture says that *"...his face did shine as the sun, and his raiment was white as the light"* (Matt. 17:2). The nature of God radiated through Jesus' entire being. Not only did His face shine, but His clothes, or His body, became white as light. We are the body of Christ. In the same way that the light of God radiated through Jesus on the Mount of Transfiguration, we need to shine like the "Son" here on the earth. One way He will radiate through us is through the operation of the gifts of the Spirit.

Craving the Gifts

We are told in 1 Corinthians 12:31 to covet earnestly the best gifts. The word *covet* means "to crave." You should crave the gifts of the Spirit more than you crave food.

I love Diet Coke. You could say that I am "supernaturally" addicted to it. You know how people have a cup of coffee every morning? Well, I have my Diet Coke every day. It's something that I have to have. One time I flew to Paris to minister. By the time the airplane landed at the Charles de Gaulle Airport, I *had* to have a Diet Coke. I ended up paying $8.00 for it, and I didn't mind one bit. When you're addicted, you're addicted!

About 15 years ago I received an invitation to minister in Estonia. I thought, *I can handle Estonia as long as I have*

Diet Coke. Just to make sure that nothing went wrong, I packed a two liter bottle in my suitcase and took it with me. Everything was going just fine until the power went out in the place where I was staying.

I didn't know when the electricity would come back on, and I thought the soda might get warm if I left it in the refrigerator. Since it was in the winter, I thought I could leave the bottle outside for the night. However, the temperature dropped below freezing; and when I went to get the bottle the next morning, it had exploded. I wept openly! I wasn't sure how I was going to make it through the rest of the trip.

I have to have my Diet Coke every day. If I don't, you do not want to be around me. I am just like somebody who hasn't had their coffee in the morning—irritable! If my flesh can crave Diet Coke, how much more should my spirit man crave the things of the Holy Spirit?

In the same way that you can become addicted to coffee, or in my case, Diet Coke, you can become addicted to the Holy Spirit. You can become so accustomed to the Holy Spirit flowing through you that you become irritable when He's not.

How many times have you gone to bed at night upset because the Holy Spirit didn't use you that day to operate in the gifts of the Spirit? Smith Wigglesworth was like that. He was known to have said, "I'm not going to sleep until I

get somebody saved." He was so accustomed to the Holy Spirit leading him to people who needed ministry that he expected it every day. He was not content to experience the power of God for himself. He *had* to be a vessel that God's power could flow through him and meet the needs of the unsaved.

You should have a burning desire to be used in the gifts of the Spirit. My prayer is that when you lie in bed at night, you can see yourself being used by the Holy Spirit. I can hear you say, "Well, that's nice, Joe. But how can the gifts of the Spirit be manifested through me? I have never even prophesied."

If you desire it, it will happen. God wants to see people set free, and He will work through anybody who makes him- or herself available. For the next seven days, I want you to pray this prayer: *"Lord, You are my Father. You said that I could ask for the gifts of the Spirit to operate in my life. I pray that You would grant that I would speak Your Word with all boldness and that through the stretching forth of my hand, You would heal and perform signs and wonders so Your name would be glorified."*

A More Excellent Way

If we are going to change our thought patterns to seek after spiritual things, then we are going to have to walk in unselfish love. In the same verse that Paul told the Corinthian church to covet the gifts of the Spirit, he writes, *"...and yet shew I unto you a more excellent way"* (1 Cor. 12:31). That way is walking in love.

When you walk in love, you are delighted in the well-being of others. You put their needs above your own and seek God to meet their needs and not yours. If we want to see the gifts of the Spirit flow through us, then we have to operate in love.

Jesus has appeared to me a couple of times over the last few years. When I looked at Him, I could see that He was the most powerful person in the universe. But what impressed me more was the love that came out of His eyes. His love gripped my heart. Love needs to be at the forefront of our thinking in the last days.

The more we are moved with compassion, the more we will see the Holy Spirit flow through us. That means setting aside past hurts, bitterness, anger, etc. It doesn't matter how long you have had to "put up" with somebody's hostility toward you. We are told to *"Love [our] enemies, do good to them which hate you, Bless them that curse you, and pray for them which despitefully use you"* (Luke 6:27,28).

If we want to see the power of God in operation, we are going to have to pray for the people who wrong us. That can be tough because the flesh always wants to retaliate. God, however, wants us to walk in the Spirit. When

we do, we will walk in the power of the Spirit in the same way that Jesus did.

Walking in love is the heartbeat of the power of God. John 13:35 says that we will be known by the love that we have for one another. You can yield yourself to the Holy Spirit and prophesy for 45 minutes, call out 20 miracles, lay hands on an entire congregation, and see everybody get healed. But if after the service was over, you were rude to people on your way out the door, they would think that you were a jerk. It wouldn't matter what God was able to do through you. If you do not walk in love, it doesn't mean anything.

The Power of the Word

Over the last 20 years we have been taught the importance of the Word of God. We don't rely on manifestations; we rely on the Word. Why? So we don't get stuck in a ditch the way the healing ministers of the 50s did. They had awesome miracles during their services, but if the Holy Ghost did not manifest, they went home.

Today, if the Holy Spirit doesn't move in a service, we keep on preaching the Word. That way people won't go home thinking it wasn't God's will for them to get healed. Anybody can get healed and delivered simply from hearing and reading the Word.

Get Ready To Be Used!

One time when Jesus was in His hometown of Nazareth, the people tried to put Him on the spot and pressure Him into "performing" miracles. As was His custom, He went to the synagogue on the Sabbath. On this day, He read from the book of Isaiah.

> *The Spirit of the Lord is upon me, because he hath anointed me to preach the gospel to the poor; he hath sent me to heal the brokenhearted, to preach deliverance to the captives, and recovering of sight to the blind, to set at liberty them that are bruised, To preach the acceptable year of the Lord.*

> LUKE 4:18,19

When he finished reading, everyone wanted to see what He was going to do. They were waiting for Him to "perform." After all, they had heard about the exploits He did throughout Israel. They wanted Him to demonstrate His power among them. However, He sat down and said, *"This day is this scripture fulfilled in your ears"* (v. 21).

Oh, did they get mad! They began to say, "Well, you know that's only Joseph's son. Don't His brothers and sisters live down the street from us? Who does He think He is?" It says in Mark 6:3 that they were offended by Him. He responded by saying:

> *Ye will surely say unto me this proverb, Physician, heal thyself: whatsoever we have heard done in Capernaum, do also here in thy country...Verily I say unto you, No prophet is accepted in his own country. But I tell you of a*

*truth, many widows were in Israel in the days of
Elias…when great famine was throughout all the land;
But unto none of them was Elias sent, save unto Sarepta, a
city of Sidon, unto a woman that was a widow. And many
lepers were in Israel in the time of Eliseus the prophet; and
none of them was cleansed, saving Naaman the Syrian.*

LUKE 4:23-27

They tried to put Jesus on the spot. If He *really* had all
this power, then why didn't He perform for them? Even
Jesus could not perform. Even though He is the Son of
God, He could not "make" the gifts of the Spirit operate.
Mark 6:5 says that *"he could there do no mighty work, save that
he laid his hands upon a few sick folk, and healed them."*

As the Spirit Wills

I have seen this same thing happen today. I've heard
people say, "Well, if healing is for today, why don't you go
heal somebody?" You can't. Just because I believe what
the Bible has to say about healing, *I* cannot heal anybody.
If the people I am praying for do not believe a word I am
saying, they are not going to get healed—that is unless the
Holy Spirit manifests Himself.

The manifestations of the Spirit are as the Spirit wills.
While you can't make the Holy Spirit do anything, you can
pray that He will manifest and be ready when He wants to

move. The book of Acts wonderfully documents the supernatural acts of the Holy Spirit flowing through the early
church. He was not particular in who He chose to move
through. He used anybody who would make him- or
herself available. God is not looking for a degree or
eloquence of speech. He is looking for availability.

You never know how the Holy Spirit will use you. You
may be lying in bed and suddenly feel an urge to pray for
somebody. When that happens, follow the urge. Get out of
bed and pray. The Holy Spirit may give you a word of
knowledge and tell you something about that person you
did not know.

In the following chapters, I am going to explain how to
recognize the voice of the Holy Spirit and how to step out
on His leadings. When you have finished reading this
book, I believe you will no longer be hesitant in obeying
the Holy Spirit's instructions. Instead, I believe you will
demonstrate a resurrection lifestyle and be a ready and
willing vessel in the end-time move of God that is about to
take place.

Chapter Six

Revealing the Future

$\mathcal{T}$he gifts of the Spirit are outlined in 1 Corinthians 12:7-10 and include the word of wisdom, the word of knowledge, the gift of special faith, the gifts of healings, the working of miracles, the gift of prophecy, the discerning of spirits, divers kinds of tongues, and the interpretation of tongues.

These gifts operate as the Spirit of God wills. That means you can't wake up in the morning and decide that you are going to prophesy to your neighbor or operate in the working of miracles. You can't choose which gifts you want to manifest on any particular day. It is up to God to give you a word of knowledge or a word of wisdom. You can, however, put yourself in a position so that you immediately respond when the Holy Spirit wants to manifest Himself.

First Corinthians 12:7 says, *"But the manifestation of the Spirit is given to every man to profit withal."* The word *manifestation* means to "make evident or certain by showing or displaying."[1] In other words, the Spirit of God wants to be seen in our lives by using one of the gifts of the Spirit.

The Holy Spirit will never "overtake" you when He wants to flow through you. You have to be willing to yield yourself to Him and do whatever He asks. If you don't yield to Him, He won't use you. If He lays it on your heart to pray for your neighbor or coworker and you ignore His leading, He won't force you.

You have to get to a point where you are willing to do whatever He asks you to do, whenever He wants you to do it. When you are willing to do His good pleasure, you will find that the Holy Spirit will call on you often.

Each of the gifts of the Spirit operates differently. We see this in the following verses.

> *Now there are diversities of gifts, but the same Spirit. And there are differences of administrations, but the same Lord. And there are diversities of operations, but it is the same God which worketh all in all.*

> 1 CORINTHIANS 12:4-6

The Holy Spirit likes diversity. I don't know that I have ever been in two services where the Spirit of God moved exactly the same way.

---

[1] Merriam-Webster Online Dictionary, www.m-w.com, s.v. manifest.

The gifts of the Spirit also operate differently through different people. That makes of sense when you think about it. Your personality will be evident in the way you operate in the gifts. When the Holy Spirit comes on you, you are not suddenly turned into a different person. A quiet person may become bolder, but you are still you. You will prophesy in the way that you talk. You don't get a new vocabulary when the Holy Spirit speaks through you in prophecy.

It has been taught in days gone by that only certain people in the body of Christ can operate in the gifts of the Spirit. That is not true. While the gifts may operate more frequently through certain people, anyone can yield to the Holy Spirit and allow Him to manifest Himself through them.

Classifications of the Gifts

There are three different classifications of the gifts of the Spirit. They are the power gifts, which include the working of miracles, the gift of faith, and the gifts of healings. These gifts do something. They demonstrate something. Next are the revelation gifts, which reveal something. They include the word of knowledge, the word of wisdom, and the discernment of spirits. Finally, we have the vocal gifts, which include divers kinds of tongues, the interpretation of tongues, and prophecy.

All of these gifts need to be in operation in the body of Christ. If the Holy Spirit is not allowed to flow freely, the church will become dead and stagnant. Throughout history you can see that every great move of God was propelled by the Holy Spirit and not by people. It was the Holy Spirit who prodded people to pray and cry out for revival. He could only work through yielded people. If nobody would yield to His urgings to pray and operate in the gifts of the Spirit, then He couldn't do anything.

Whether or not God uses me, I want to be in the middle of whatever He is doing. It's wonderful to see the working of miracles and the gifts of special faith in operation; but I do not want to just watch what's going on. I want to be an active participant.

Given by God

"For to one is given by the Spirit the word of wisdom; to another the word of knowledge by the same Spirit" (1 Cor. 12:8).

Notice that it says, *"For to one is given...."* No one operates in all of the gifts, all of the time. I've heard people say, "I possess the gift of the word of knowledge." Nobody really *possesses* any of the gifts of the Spirit.

For instance, I possess a Bible. It's mine. I could give it away because I own it. I can't give anybody one of the gifts of the Spirit. They are not mine to give. They are ministry tools given by the Spirit of God, and they operate as the Spirit wills.

First Corinthians 12:11 says, *"But all these worketh that one and the selfsame Spirit, dividing to every man severally as he will."* God can work through anybody He desires. Jesus is the administrator of the gifts of the Spirit, and the Holy Spirit reveals them.

At any given time, Jesus could say He wants to do something through a certain person. The Holy Spirit then nudges that brother or sister to respond. The moment the individual yields to the Holy Spirit, He can manifest Himself.

Aren't you ready for the Holy Spirit to do some work in the earth? More and more, we are seeing movies and television series that showcase the devil's power through witchcraft, mediums, and spirits. The world believes in astrologers and thinks that the devil has power. God has more power than they ever dreamed of. When Christians finally begin to yield to the Spirit, we will finally see the awesome power of God demonstrated like never before.

The Word of Wisdom

Let's take a look at how the Holy Spirit operates through the revelation gifts. We will begin with the word of wisdom. The definition of *the word of wisdom* is "the

supernatural revelation by the Spirit of God concerning the divine purpose in the mind and will of God."

A word of wisdom always reveals something about the future. Sometimes when we hear a prophecy, what we are really hearing is a word of wisdom using the vehicle of prophecy.

The best example of a word of wisdom is the book of Revelations. That book is a word of knowledge and a word of wisdom. The first part of Revelations is a word of knowledge. These chapters reveal what is currently going on in the church. The remaining chapters of the book are one long, continuous word of wisdom. They contain facts about things that have not yet taken place.

One of the first examples in the early church of how the word of wisdom operates is found in Acts 9. Not long after Jesus ascended into heaven, the early church experienced severe persecution. Many Christians were arrested and put in jail for preaching the Gospel.

Their main antagonist was a young man named Saul. One day Jesus appeared to Ananias in the form of a vision and told him where to find Saul. He told him that Saul was blind and that He wanted Ananias to lay hands on him so he would receive his sight.

The Scripture doesn't call Ananias a prophet or an apostle. He was what I call common folk. He was somebody who gave his life to Christ after the ascension of Jesus.

Ananias argued with Jesus. He didn't want to go anywhere near this man. After all, Saul was one of the main reasons why Christians in the early church were running for their lives. Jesus' answer to Ananias was actually a word of wisdom. It was supernatural insight into the future.

But the Lord said unto him, Go thy way: for he is a chosen vessel unto me, to bear my name before the Gentiles, and kings, and the children of Israel: For I will shew him how great things he must suffer for my name's sake.

ACTS 9:15,16

There were actually three revelation gifts in operation in this situation. First, the discerning of spirits operated. Ananias saw Jesus. Second, a word of knowledge. Jesus told Ananias where Saul was. And finally, a word of wisdom. Ananias was told what was going to happen to Paul in the future.

Anytime the Holy Spirit manifests Himself, it's always to accomplish something. I love church services where I get goose bumps. But if that's the only thing that happens, then the Holy Spirit wasn't able to achieve what He wanted to do. The Holy Spirit manifests Himself so He can affect people's lives.

That is also the reason why we are here. Every Christian ought to affect the lives of people around them. I want to be proficient in the operations of the Holy Spirit so

I can help people, not so I can brag about having a word of wisdom or a word of knowledge.

Being Forewarned

Here is another example of the word of wisdom operating. We see that the Holy Spirit warned Paul of what was going to happen to him.

> *And as we tarried there many days, there came down from Judaea a certain prophet, named Agabus. And when he was come unto us, he took Paul's girdle, and bound his own hands and feet, and said, Thus saith the Holy Ghost, So shall the Jews at Jerusalem bind the man that owneth this girdle, and shall deliver him into the hands of the Gentiles. And when we heard these things, both we, and they of that place, besought him not to go up to Jerusalem. Then Paul answered, What mean ye to weep and to break mine heart? for I am ready not to be bound only, but also to die at Jerusalem for the name of the Lord Jesus. And when he would not be persuaded, we ceased, saying, The will of the Lord be done.*
>
> ACTS 21:10-14

I don't believe Agabus woke up that morning expecting to prophesy to Paul. I think that when he walked into the room, the Holy Spirit led him to pick up Paul's girdle and bind him with it. The *Amplified Bible* translates the word *girdle* as "belt." Agabus took Paul's belt and tied him up with it.

In this example, the Holy Spirit acted out the word of wisdom for them. He showed them what the future held for Paul. Some people say that Agabus prophesied doom over Paul. No, the Holy Spirit warned Paul of what was ahead of him. Thank God that the Holy Spirit can warn us about the future.

One time toward the end of a service after I had laid hands on people, I wanted to rest for a minute. As I was walking toward my chair, I had a word of wisdom in a vision. I saw a man walk up to the pastor of the church where I was ministering and take a swing at him. The pastor was able to jump back and the swing just missed him.

I thought, *Dear Lord, what in the world was that?* I said, "Lord, should I say something now, or should I wait until after the service to talk to the pastor."

You have to realize that just because the Lord shows you something, He doesn't always want you to say anything to anybody. I once had a word of knowledge that I held for six months before I was allowed to speak it. In this case the Lord said, "Go ahead and give it out."

I said, "Pastor, if this means anything to you, God is trying to warn you. If it doesn't, I missed it." I then told him what I saw. He simply said, "Praise God."

About four months later, the pastor called to tell me that a man in his church came against him and tried to do everything in his power to destroy the church. Things had gotten pretty rough. One of the men in the congregation remembered what I had said and reminded the pastor.

It was evident then that this had been a true word from God, and it helped the pastor when he realized that God had warned him four months earlier. You never know how you may be able to help someone when you yield to the Holy Spirit.

It's also important that when somebody gives you a word, you receive it as though God had said it to you. At the time I gave this word to the pastor, it did not mean anything to him. He simply put it on a shelf. It wasn't until months later that it helped him, especially when he remembered the part that the man was not able to hit him.

Being Forewarned Through Dreams

You don't operate in the gifts through your natural abilities; they are supernatural. The word of wisdom is not natural wisdom. Although some people are very smart and make wise choices throughout their lives, a word of wisdom is always supernatural insight about a future event.

Notice that it is called a "word" of wisdom. That means you are only getting a fragment of what you need to know.

I wish I had received more information for that pastor, but all I received was a small portion of what would happen.

The Lord wants to warn His people before tragedy strikes. He told the prophet Agabus that a great famine was coming throughout the earth (Acts 11:28 NKJV), and they weren't caught off guard. They knew what to do beforehand.

I once had a dream that the pastor of the church I attend in Tulsa was in a plane crash. In the dream I saw people pulling him out of the plane after his twin-engine airplane had crashed. He was cut up and badly bruised. I saw him lay his hand on his head and command his body to be well. I woke with a start and began praying that this would not happen. At that time, I did not feel led to tell him about the dream. I just felt that I was supposed to pray.

I am convinced that people around the globe were also praying. Sometimes I think I'm so clueless that God had to give me a dream to get me to pray. If I had been more sensitive to the Holy Spirit, He could have just said, "Joe, I need you to pray for your pastor." Instead, He had to manifest Himself in a word of wisdom.

The dream later became a reality. Both engines failed as my pastor was taking off. The plane crashed at the end of the runway and skidded to the edge of a cliff. It was a miracle that the plane did not go over the cliff. It stopped at the very edge, and his life was spared.

The Lord knows what is going to happen in the future. He will always do anything He can to warn us of danger. It's up to us to be sensitive to the Holy Spirit to hear His warnings.

Confirmation Through Visions

The word of wisdom is not limited to giving warnings to people. It can also confirm what you are supposed to do.

I was ministering in a Pentecostal church in Pittsville, Illinois, when I had a vision. I saw children running down the middle aisle of a church. I thought, *My goodness! Children!* The service was just about over, but I did not feel that I was supposed to tell the entire congregation. After the service, I was scheduled to go out to lunch with the pastor, and I thought I would tell him what I saw then.

While we were eating lunch, I said to him, "You know, I had the strangest thing happen during the service. If it means something to you, wonderful! If it doesn't, I missed it. I saw children running up and down the middle aisle of the church. They were playing and having a great time."

He told me that they were going to build a new church adjacent to the present building. He had been praying about what to do with the current sanctuary. He had been thinking about turning it into a building for the children to use, but he was not sure if he was making the right decision.

That was a word of wisdom for the pastor. He put a demand on the Holy Spirit and was shown what to do. I'm glad that God will get involved in our lives and help us out in both big and little decisions. I would much rather have Him involved in my life than trying to figure everything by myself.

Discerning the Truth From the False

It was common for the early church to operate in the supernatural. To them, it was normal. Nobody made a big deal about having a word of knowledge or a word of wisdom.

We are coming to a time where we are going to see a flood of the gifts of the Spirit in operation. Unfortunately, we are also going to see a lot of stuff that is not from God. We need to be able to tell the difference between the two. Whenever there is a move of God, the devil does not want to be left out. He will quickly institute a counterfeit and try to get people to follow him instead of God.

Jesus talked about the end times and warned His disciples to beware of false prophets. *"For false Christs and false prophets shall rise, and shall shew signs and wonders, to seduce, if it were possible, even the elect"* (Mark 13:22).

This is why it's important to go to a church that not only teaches sound doctrine, but one that also moves in the gifts of the Spirit. When you see your pastor operating in the gifts of the Spirit week after week, you will be able to recognize when you see something that is not of God.

The way to recognize anything counterfeit, whether it is money or the move of God, is to become familiar with the real thing. When you come in contact with the counterfeit, it won't sit well with your spirit and you will intuitively know that it is not of God.

People sometimes get off and get weird in the things of the Spirit. But that does not mean you should refuse to operate in any of the gifts because of that. You should never back down from what God wants to do in someone's life. I have seen counterfeit money, but I would never dream of throwing out my "real" money. No, just don't get involved in the counterfeit.

As you step out in the gifts of the Spirit, you will also be able to share with others how to operate in the Spirit the "right" way. If you sit back and don't do anything, you enable the devil to spread false teachings among those who are ignorant in the things of God.

Chapter Seven

Reading People's Mail

*T*he human body is amazing, and many books have been written about how it works. One thing that none of the medical textbooks acknowledge is that man is a tri-part being, made up of a spirit, soul, and body.

The Holy Spirit dwells in your spirit. When He wants to communicate to you, He speaks to your spirit. Your spirit is influenced by your soul, which is comprised of your mind, will, and emotions. The more sensitive your spirit is to the things of God and the more your soul is renewed to the Word, the better you will be able to hear what the Holy Spirit is saying to you.

Your soul is the gateway to your heart, or your spirit man. What you hear and see must first be filtered through your mind, will, and emotions. It is up to you to choose what you allow into your heart. If you have placed a guard on your heart, you won't listen to or look at things that are garbage, which include fear, sex, lust, anger, bitterness, etc. However, if you allow your soul to feed on garbage, it will be harder for you to hear the Holy Spirit's voice.

On the other hand, the more you feed on godly things—the Word of God, Christian books, CDs, and tapes—the easier it will be for your spirit man to be in control. That is why you are told in Proverbs 4:23 to guard your heart with all diligence, for out of it flow the issues of life. If you don't do this and your flesh is in control, God will have to work that much harder to get your attention when the Holy Spirit wants to speak to you.

Finding Out What's Going On

A word of knowledge is "a supernatural revelation by the Spirit of God concerning facts about people, places, and things." It normally concerns something in the present or past.

There are many examples in the Bible of the word of wisdom and the word of knowledge operating together. While they are separate and distinct gifts, they can operate at the same time.

A good example of a word of knowledge is found in the book of Acts. When Jesus appeared to Ananias in a vision concerning Saul of Tarsus, He gave him a word of knowledge.

And there was a certain disciple at Damascus, named Ananias; and to him said the Lord in a vision, Ananias. And he said, Behold, I am here, Lord. And the Lord said

unto him, Arise, and go into the street which is called
Straight, and enquire in the house of Judas for one called
Saul, of Tarsus: for, behold, he prayeth, And hath seen in a
vision a man named Ananias coming in, and putting his
hand on him, that he might receive his sight.

ACTS 9:10-12

Jesus wanted Ananias to pray for Saul of Tarsus.
Before he could do this, he had to know where to go. Jesus
gave Ananias supernatural knowledge concerning Saul's
whereabouts. He could not have known in the natural
where he was, and with Saul's reputation, I'm sure that he
did not want to know.

Usually when the Holy Spirit gives me a word of
knowledge, it is not for me but for somebody else. One day,
however, I received a word of knowledge about my situation. I had recently bought a new car and was trying to
start it. I couldn't get the engine to crank, and the Lord
said, "You're out of gas."

I sat there arguing with Him. "Oh no, I'm not out of gas.
This is a brand-new car!" Since *I* knew better, I had the
car towed to the dealership. They looked it over and told
me that I was out of gas! If I had only listened to the Holy
Spirit, I could have saved myself a lot of time and money.

I love it when the Holy Spirit reads somebody's mail
through a word of knowledge. I was in a church in
Willimantic, Connecticut, and the Lord gave me a word of

knowledge about that church's new building. When I told
the people what the Lord showed me, it confirmed to the
congregation that the pastor was doing the right thing
about the land and the building.

Nathanael's Call

When Jesus called His disciples, He simply told most
of them to follow Him. In the case of Nathanael, the word
of knowledge was in operation.

> *Philip findeth Nathanael, and saith unto him, We have
> found him, of whom Moses in the law, and the prophets, did
> write, Jesus of Nazareth, the son of Joseph. And Nathanael
> said unto him, Can there any good thing come out of
> Nazareth? Philip saith unto him, Come and see. Jesus saw
> Nathanael coming to him, and saith of him, Behold an
> Israelite indeed, in whom is no guile! Nathanael saith unto
> him, Whence knowest thou me? Jesus answered and said
> unto him, Before that Philip called thee, when thou wast
> under the fig tree, I saw thee. Nathanael answered and
> saith unto him, Rabbi, thou art the Son of God; thou art
> the King of Israel.*

JOHN 1:45-49

Jesus was not all knowing when He walked on the
earth. He had to depend on the Holy Spirit in the same
way you and I have to. He sensed that Nathanael should
be a part of His team, but Nathanael needed to be

convinced to follow Jesus. If Jesus would have walked up to him and said, "Follow me," he probably would not have. Because the Holy Spirit manifested in the form of a word of knowledge, Jesus was able to grab Nathanael's attention. The plan and purpose of God needed to be fulfilled, and the Holy Spirit orchestrated the events so Nathanael would follow that plan.

Anytime, Anywhere

The manifestations of the Spirit aren't limited to church services. The book of Acts is filled with examples of the gifts of the Spirit manifesting outside of the church. The Holy Spirit can speak to you anytime and anywhere. You can be at home, in the office, driving your car, or on the phone. Because the Holy Spirit dwells in you, the power of God can literally show up anywhere you go.

A lady in Colorado once shared with me how she received a word of knowledge on her job. She worked with a woman who didn't like her and who constantly harassed her on the job. One day the Holy Spirit told the church lady that her coworker had hurt her thumb. She said to the woman, "The Lord told me that something was wrong with your hand. Is it okay?"

The woman's eyes got really wide and she said, "How did you know that I hurt my hand? I didn't tell anybody!"

"The Lord told me," the church lady said. "Do you mind if I pray for you?"

When she prayed, God healed the woman's hand, right there at work! This woman had been harassing the church lady for years. A word of knowledge got her attention, and she became open to the Gospel. She also stopped harassing the church lady.

This is a great example of how God wants all Christians to allow the power of God to flow through them and minister to others regardless of what is said or done to them. The church lady could have tried to avoid all contact with this woman. But instead, she was an unselfish vessel who was used mightily by God to demonstrate His love.

On the Road

Many years ago, I worked for a minister and was what you would call a "shoeshine guy." That means I did whatever he needed me to do. He and two other ministers were preaching at a weeklong campmeeting, and I was there to serve.

Before the first service, I had a vision in my hotel room while I was studying and praying. I saw a car accident, and I watched as something hit a woman on the back of her head. When the object hit her, she collapsed in the car. Then, I saw a man working at what looked like a sawmill.

He was hauling wood when a huge log rolled off the truck and hit him in the middle of his back.

I was excited about what I had seen and expected God to heal these people at the evening service. I thought the minister would call these things out that night. When it didn't happen, I assumed that He had missed it. When these words of knowledge didn't get called out the second night of the campmeeting, I thought that maybe I missed it. Many people were healed at the services but not the two people that I saw.

On the third night of the campmeeting, the man I had been traveling with told me he had to leave early and that I needed to preach for him in the morning session. I said, "What? No way. I'm not preaching tomorrow morning. You are preaching tomorrow." I wasn't expecting to speak and was actually thrilled that I wasn't.

He said, "No, you're preaching."

Since it was my job to do whatever needed to be done, I stood in back of the pulpit the next morning and attempted to deliver a message. I don't know if you could call what I did preaching. In fact, a lady came up to me afterward and asked, "You don't do this for a living, do you?" It was pretty bad. I did not want to preach and it showed!

I was a shoeshine guy without any polish, but God loves people so much that He used me in spite of my inabilities. At the end of my message, I thought, *Well, let me call*

out those things that I saw earlier in the week. I didn't know what else to do.

I said, "I had a vision on Monday. I saw a lady in a car wreck, and I saw something hit the back of your neck." A woman jumped up and ran as fast as she could to the altar. When I laid hands on her, she was instantly healed.

Then I relayed the second vision. "I saw a man, and I saw a big log. I don't know if you are a lumberjack, but I saw a log hit you in the middle of your back. God wants to heal you right now." A man came forward and said that what I saw had happened to him. He had been in pain for many years. He, too, was instantly healed.

I am so glad the Holy Spirit is not looking for degrees and polished messages. He is looking for people who are willing to be vessels He can flow through. It did not matter that I stumbled through my message. He still showed up that day. I am so glad He did; it would have been a real disaster if He didn't.

If you will just be ready for it, the revelation gifts will regularly operate in you. We are coming to a time where you may have many words of knowledge in one day. Never take it lightly when the Lord shows you something about somebody. Maybe you're supposed to share what you saw with them and maybe you're not. The important thing is to always be obedient to whatever God instructs you to do.

The Judgment Side of the Gifts

While most people are familiar with a minister calling out different ailments in a church service, the Bible also records examples of the Holy Spirit revealing sin.

Do you remember the story of Naaman, the leper? Naaman was a captain in the Syrian army who was stricken with leprosy. He came to Elisha to get healed and was told to dip in the Jordan River seven times. After following the prophet's instructions, he was healed of the leprosy.

He was so thrilled to be healed that he wanted to bless Elisha with money and clothes. Elisha wanted Naaman to know there was a God in Israel who was able to heal and refused to accept his gifts.

After Naaman left, Elisha's servant, Gehazi, snuck out of the camp and followed him. When he was far enough away so Elisha could not see what he was doing, Gehazi approached Naaman and said, "You know, we just had some visitors drop in, and we could use some of your gifts after all."

Naaman was glad to help and even gave Gehazi more than what he had asked for. When the servant got back to the camp, Elisha asked, "Where have you been, Gehazi?"

"I haven't been anywhere," the servant replied.

Elisha, however, had received a word of knowledge and knew exactly what Gehazi did. He said,

*Went not mine heart with thee, when the man turned again
from his chariot to meet thee? Is it a time to receive money,
and to receive garments, and oliveyards, and vineyards, and
sheep, and oxen, and menservants, and maidservants? The
leprosy therefore of Naaman shall cleave unto thee....*

2 Kings 5:26,27

Elisha did not watch Gehazi through a telescope when
he left the camp. The Spirit of God showed him know
exactly what the wicked servant was up to. Talk about
getting somebody's attention!

In the last days, we will see the gifts of the Spirit manifest in the form of judgment. People are no longer going to
be able to get away with secret sin. God is going to reveal
the hidden things and judgment will come on both
Christians and non-Christians. When it starts happening,
people will realize that God sees what they are doing even
when they don't think anybody is watching.

You do not have to fall under the hand of judgment. It
will be the things that you don't judge yourself of that will
cause your downfall. So let go of the weights and
hindrances that are keeping you from fully serving the
Lord. You can be assured that if you judge yourself and
guard what you allow to enter your heart, you will never
have a Gehazi experience.

Chapter Eight

Seeing Into the Spirit Realm

A church that is not operating in the supernatural is superficial and has been reduced to a social club. If we want to stop the works of the devil, we need to have an imprint of the supernatural on our lives.

I do not want to be involved in a dead religion. I want to serve a God who hears me when I pray and who can save, heal, and deliver. The main difference between Christianity and other religions is that we worship a God who is alive and who deeply cares about our well-being.

First Corinthians 12:2 says, *"Ye know that ye were Gentiles, carried away unto these dumb idols, even as ye were led."* Many people throughout the earth worship idols that cannot speak. They pray to Buddha, any one of the many Hindu gods, and to Allah; but their prayers never go beyond the room they are in.

Not only can we pray to Jehovah, but He will also speak to us. If we will take the time and quiet ourselves and listen, we will find that the Holy Spirit is speaking all

the time. He will warn us of impending danger, give us wisdom in difficult situations, and guide us into all truth. And through the discerning of spirits, we can also see into the spirit realm.

Go South, Young Man

The discerning of spirits is not a spirit of discernment. Women are particularly good at sensing things. When meeting someone or learning of a situation, they can immediately tell if something is not right. We call it women's intuition.

But just because somebody is perceptive in the natural does not mean the individual is perceptive spiritually. Discerning of spirits is not keen spiritual perception. *Discern* means "to see into the spirit realm."

We are coming to a time in the last days where entire congregations will be able to see into the spirit realm. I believe they will be able to see angels as they minister to the needs of the people in church services.

An example of an angel manifesting himself in the early church is found in Acts 8:26. *"And the angel of the Lord spake unto Philip, saying, Arise, and go toward the south unto the way that goeth down from Jerusalem unto Gaza, which is desert."* The discerning of spirits was in operation here because Philip saw the angel.

The angel gave Philip instructions on what he needed to do. Notice that the angel didn't give him elaborate instructions. He only told him to start traveling south. He didn't say, "Take Highway 60 south until you reach Beersheba. Then get on Highway 40 until you pass a group of palm trees on the left-hand side of the road. There you will see a man...."

No, he just said, "Pack your bags and head south." After Philip obediently followed the angel's instructions, the Holy Spirit told him to *"Go near, and join thyself to this chariot"* (v. 29). If Philip would have ignored the angel, he would not have been in position to hear the voice of the Holy Spirit.

What was the end result of this manifestation of the discerning of spirits and the word of wisdom? An Ethiopian eunuch got saved. While that may not seem too significant, the salvation of this one man is more far-reaching than is recorded in the Scripture.

His salvation led to a large number of Jews in Ethiopia converting to Christianity. Throughout the centuries, their ancestors have kept many of the Jewish traditions and beliefs with one exception: They believe in Jesus. More recently, around 80,000 Ethiopian Jews returned to their homeland of Israel in the 1990s.

This is an excellent example of why you need to be full of the Holy Spirit. Just think if Philip would have missed

it. He could have thought that he had a little too much wine that day and ignored the vague instructions of the angel. The fruit of his obedience is evident today in the Ethiopian Jewish believers who have firmly placed their trust in the Lord Jesus Christ.

The End of Time

Some of the most amazing biblical examples we have of the discerning of spirits involve the visions the apostle John and the prophets of the Old Testament had concerning the end of this age. John had a front row seat when he recorded the panoramic vision of the destruction that awaits mankind in the book of Revelation.

Daniel also saw into the spirit realm concerning the day in which we now live. The Bible records that he had visions even when he was with other people. *"And I Daniel alone saw the vision: for the men that were with me saw not the vision; but a great quaking fell upon them, so that they fled to hide themselves"* (Daniel 10:7).

The prophet Ezekiel also caught peeks into the spirit realm concerning the end of the age. Probably the most glorious glimpse into the spirit realm was when Isaiah saw the throne of God.

> *In the year that king Uzziah died I saw also the Lord sitting upon a throne, high and lifted up, and his train*

filled the temple. Above it stood the seraphims: each one had six wings; with twain he covered his face, and with twain he covered his feet, and with twain he did fly. And one cried unto another, and said, Holy, holy, holy, is the Lord of hosts: the whole earth is full of his glory.

ISAIAH 6:1-3

Seeing Into the Spirit Realm

I remember the first time the discerning of spirits operated in my life. I traveled with the minister I worked for to New England. During the service, he was laying hands on people.

I was minding my own business and was not expecting what happened next. Whenever my eyes have been open to the spirit realm, I was never expecting anything to happen. It just happened.

I looked up, and all of a sudden I saw into the spirit realm. I could barely see the minister as he was laying hands on people in the healing line. Surrounding the people were big, white, tall angels that glowed with the glory of God. They were catching people as they were slain in the spirit.

One angel followed the minister wherever he went. Every move that the minister made, he made too. As I was

watching everything that was going on, one of the angels turned around and smiled at me.

Now, from the time that I was a child, my mother pumped the Word in me. I knew all about angels and believed in their existence, but I never expected anything like this to happen to me. It scared me so bad, I almost left the building!

Since then, I probably have seen into the spirit realm 150 times. I have almost always seen angels. Less than one percent of the time did I see evil spirits. If somebody ever tells you that they see devils on you, be careful. The discerning of spirits is not always to discern devils. I have only seen evil spirits three times.

The closer we get to Jesus' return, the more frequently these things are going to happen. Get ready. You never know when an angel will appear to you. If you begin to prepare yourself now, maybe you won't freak out the way I did!

One time I was in a prayer meeting, and a man stood up to speak. As soon as he opened his mouth, I knew he wasn't of God. Everything he said was unscriptural. As he was talking, I saw into the spirit realm. I saw two evil spirits standing on his shoulders. The imps would whisper into his ears, and he would repeat everything they said.

In cases like this, you do not need to see into the spirit realm to know that what a person says is unscriptural. You don't have to wait for the discerning of spirits to manifest when you have the Word. It is the plumb line by which you judge what is said and what you see.

A Visit From Jesus

Another time I saw into the spirit realm was when I was preparing to minister at a campmeeting. One night as I was lying in bed, I had a burden to pray for the upcoming meetings. My wife was asleep, and I didn't want to wake her, so I got out of bed and walked into the master bathroom.

When I stepped into the bathroom, Jesus appeared to me and told me certain things I needed to do during the campmeeting. Notice that He didn't appear to me to talk about how things were going. He had a specific purpose for appearing to me.

He first spoke to me about several things in my ministry. Then He began to talk about the upcoming campmeeting as well as the church that was holding the meeting.

As soon as He began talking about campmeeting, I had a vision of the service. Jesus entered the sanctuary through a side door and walked up to the different speakers. He spoke to each of them individually.

After that, it was over. Jesus had disappeared, and I was back in my bathroom. I walked to my bed and began

to cry like a baby. The love I saw in His face had gripped my heart.

At campmeeting, I was scheduled to speak at the afternoon meeting. I didn't know if I would see Jesus walk through the side door of the building as He did in the vision. When I stood on the platform, I noticed that the ministers were sitting exactly as I had seen them in the vision.

I never experienced an anointing as powerfully as I did that day. It was so strong I could hardly stand up. I thought, *Lord, what's going to happen? A month ago, I saw You walk in and talk to the ministers.* He said, "You're going to have to tell them what you saw Me say to them."

I would have preferred that He would have manifested to each of the ministers Himself. It would have carried a lot more weight than my telling them what I saw.

We are the Lord's mouthpiece on this earth, so I walked over to the ministers and told them what I had seen a month earlier. I gave each one of them a word of knowledge about their ministry, and then I had a word of wisdom for the church that was hosting the campmeeting.

This was a manifestation of the discerning of spirits, the word of knowledge, and the word of wisdom all working together to accomplish God's will on the earth. Everything that the Lord said to that church and to the ministers has come to pass.

Start Expecting To Be Used

Don't you know if Jesus would appear to a guy like me, then He must be in a hurry to get the job done and come back for the church? He wants to use all of us. Get ready for the revelation gifts to begin manifesting in your life. Start expecting the word of knowledge, the word of wisdom, and the discerning of spirits to begin operating as easily as you pray in tongues. God wants to reveal some things to you.

I like to know things ahead of time. I'm the type of person who wants to know the end of the movie first. I always read the last chapter of a book before chapter one. I don't like to be caught off guard.

The body of Christ, however, will catch the devil off guard when we start operating in the supernatural. The devil thought he had us right where he wanted us—operating in a lackadaisical attitude toward the things of God.

You will probably throw your family members off guard when you start walking in the supernatural. They won't know what to make of you when you operate in the power and authority of God. One thing is for sure; it will grab their attention and make them more receptive to follow after the will of God for their lives.

In 1911, Marie Woodworth Edder was in Dallas, Texas. The front page of the *Dallas Times Herald* read "Put

down your umbrellas, boys. Come out there. God is healing the sick just like in the days of the Apostles."

Even though what God did during the healing revival at the beginning of the 20th Century was spectacular, it will pale in comparison to what God wants to do before Jesus' return.

I can't yell it loud enough. *GET READY FOR THE MOVE OF GOD THAT IS COMING ON THIS EARTH!* We are going to see an outbreak of people raised from the dead, and it will be noised all over the earth. We will see people translated from one place to another place.

Those who don't know the Lord will wonder, *What in the world is going on?* That will be your opportunity to share the Word of God with them and help to bring in the great harvest before the return of the Lord. Let's get ready!

Chapter Nine

Unstoppable Faith

When children ask their parents for something, most parents don't tell them to leave them alone and go away. The normal response, especially when they pull on your leg a couple of times, is "What do you want?" Whenever my daughter Lauren tells me she wants me to buy her something, I'll say, "Okay," and make a mental note to get the item at some time. If she asks again, I know she is serious. I will do whatever I can to give her what she wants.

What do you think God is going to do when you ask for the gifts of the Spirit? He is going to make sure you get them. We are right in the middle of what God wants to do before the Rapture of the church.

It is His good pleasure to cause the gifts of the Spirit to manifest in our lives. As they do, we can expect to see even greater things happen than when Jesus walked on the earth. I want more, don't you? I don't want a little bit; I want everything that God has for me.

The Power Gifts

The three power gifts include the gift of faith or special faith, the gifts of healings, and the working of miracles. The purpose of these gifts is to demonstrate that Jesus is alive.

The power gifts are my favorites. I like power. One time during a campmeeting, the power of God came on me so strongly that I fell off the platform as I was laying hands on people. I guess the Holy Spirit gave me too much power! That's probably why Jesus had the Spirit *without* measure and we have it *with* measure. We can't handle too much power or we will short-circuit.

Three Types of Faith

There are three types of faith mentioned in the Bible. The first is general faith. This is the faith that enables you to get saved. Ephesians 2:6 says, *"For by grace are ye saved through faith; and that not of yourselves: it is the gift of God."*

Another way general faith is used is when you are believing God for something. Mark 11:24 says, *"What things soever ye desire, when ye pray, believe that ye receive them, and ye shall have them."* This faith is for you personally and not for someone else.

General faith comes by hearing the Word of God. (Rom. 10:17.) You can't pray and ask God to give you faith. You must read and study the Word and then act on what you have read to develop this type of faith.

Another type of faith is the fruit of faith found in Galatians 5:22. This is actually one of the fruits of the Spirit. The fruit of faith is not really faith but faithfulness.

Faithfulness is something that is cultivated. We cannot ask God to give us faithfulness. It is up to each of us to develop it in our lives, and we will have many opportunities throughout our lives to do so.

It is possible for people to exhibit the fruit of the Spirit but not operate in the power of the Spirit. It can also be the other way around. You can operate in the power gifts but not in the fruit of the Spirit.

That is why in the healing revival of the 50s, great miracles manifested through ministers who were drunk-ards. God wants you to operate in both the fruit and power of the Spirit. When this happens, we will have one big blowout.

The third type of faith is the gift of faith. It is like a cloak that comes on you when you do not have any author-ity in a person's life. If people are closed to what you are saying when you are ministering to them, sometimes the Holy Spirit can manifest and bless them if you can get them to shift to a neutral position.

Loving the Unlovable

I have seen the gift of faith work for people who don't believe at all. I have even seen it work for people who came to church mad as a hornet. They did not want to be there but somebody drug them to church.

Suddenly the Holy Spirit manifested, and something miraculous happened in their lives. This is very typical of the Lord. Sometimes He does things for people who do not even care that He exists.

If it were up to me, I probably would not do anything for these types of people—their attitudes are so bad. It really amazes me when the Holy Spirit heals nasty people. I had one woman who came to one of my services that had been mean all of her life. The Holy Spirit manifested during the service and healed her of arthritis.

Did you ever wonder why God does such nice things for some of the most hateful people around? God loves people, and He does not want to see anybody perish. The Holy Spirit has the heart of God, and He manifests so they will know that God loves them.

Aren't you glad the Lord is in charge instead of us? If it were up to most of us, we would only ask the Holy Spirit to manifest for the people who are nice to us!

The Power Gift of Faith

The definition for the *gift of faith*, or *special* faith, is "believing God in such a way that He honors your word as His own and miraculously brings to pass what you say."

The gift of special faith is received passively in the same way you believe God passively. For instance, if I hurt my hand, I would pray, "Father, I thank You for healing my hand. I receive my healing in Jesus' name."

I did not have to *work* to get healed; I just *received* what Jesus did on the Cross 2,000 years ago. That is why I call it passive. The gift of faith is passive, because you only have to receive it when it comes on you. You cannot do anything to "make" it work.

Here is one of the first examples of the manifestation of the gift of faith that occurred in the early church.

Now Peter and John went up together into the temple at the hour of prayer, being the ninth hour. And a certain man lame from his mother's womb was carried, whom they laid daily at the gate of the temple which is called Beautiful, to ask alms of them that entered into the temple; Who seeing Peter and John about to go into the temple asked an alms. And Peter, fastening his eyes upon him with John, said, Look on us. And he gave heed unto them, expecting to receive something of them. Then Peter said, Silver and gold have I none; but such as I have give I thee: In the name of Jesus Christ of Nazareth rise up and walk. And he took

him by the right hand, and lifted him up: and immediately
his feet and ankle bones received strength. And he leaping
up stood, and walked, and entered with them into the
temple, walking, and leaping, and praising God. And all
the people saw him walking and praising God.

ACTS 3:1-9

Peter's and John's faith did not heal the lame man. This was an injection of the Holy Spirit's power. The two apostles had walked by the lame man every day on their way to the synagogue without any manifestation of the Spirit. On this particular day, they were injected with special faith, and their faith would not be denied.

The moment Peter said, *"...such as I have give I thee,"* God instantly brought his words to pass. Peter had to yield to the Holy Spirit and speak out that man's miracle. The lame man would have laid there until he died if Peter would not have yielded to the Spirit. When he spoke, it was as though God Himself performed the miracle.

Notice what Peter and John said in verse 4, *"Look on us...."* Why? They had something. When the gift of special faith came on them, they had something to give. Only a few verses later, Peter said, *"Ye men of Israel, why marvel ye at this? or why look ye so earnestly on us, as though by our own power or holiness we had made this man to walk?"* (v. 12).

He told the lame man to "Look on us," and now he is saying, "Why are you looking on us?" His question is not

as contradictory as it may sound. Peter had to get that man's attention before God could move in his life. As soon as he got it, the man's focus then had to shift to Jesus.

Because of this one miracle, 5,000 men got saved. (Acts 4:4.) This is also an example of what should be happening today. God wants to use the gifts of the Spirit to get people's attention. And when He does, we are going to see thousands of people giving their lives to Christ at one time.

Another example of the gift of faith is found in Acts 9.

> *And it came to pass, as Peter passed throughout all quarters, he came down also to the saints which dwelt at Lydda. And there he found a certain man named Aeneas, which had kept his bed eight years, and was sick of the palsy. And Peter said unto him, Aeneas, Jesus Christ maketh thee whole: arise, and make thy bed. And he arose immediately. And all that dwelt at Lydda and Saron saw him, and turned to the Lord.*
>
> ACTS 9:32,33

Notice what happened when Aeneas was healed. Everybody who lived in the towns of Lydda and Saron gave their lives to the Lord. The fruit of the gifts of the Spirit are people getting saved and drawn closer to Jesus.

The Boldness of God

You will find that when the Spirit of God comes on you, you will say things that will shock you. I have said

some things that have caused me to turn around and ask, "My Lord, who said that? Surely that didn't come out of my mouth!"

It came out so fast that I did not know where it came from. It was probably good that it happened like that. If I had time to think about it, I probably would not have said anything.

One time I was ministering in Terre Haute, Indiana. After I had preached the Word, I was laying hands on people. A young girl who had a speech impediment came to the altar. I really get mad when I see the devil harass little kids.

As I was laying my hands on her, I could tell that she was not receiving. I could sense a tangible anointing, but it was not going into her.

I perceived by the Spirit that her family had not been coming to church that much. I could see by the looks on their faces that they did not understand what we were doing.

I was about to lay hands on the next person in line when the gift of faith came on me. I turned back to the young girl and said, "In two weeks time, you will be perfectly whole!" I then continued laying hands on people, but my mind was freaking out. I thought, *Oh, my God! What did I just say?*

Thank God it wasn't me making that declaration; it was the Holy Spirit speaking through me. Two weeks later the pastor called to tell me that the little girl had been healed of the speech impediment and could speak perfectly.

We cannot force our faith on another person's will. We can agree with them in prayer according to Matthew 18:19. The prayer of agreement only works, however, when both parties have faith to receive the answer. If one person says that he or she believes, but really does not, the prayer will not get answered.

The early church was known for its boldness not its coldness. How did they get to be so bold? They were "full" of the Holy Spirit.

When you are full of the Holy Spirit, your confidence in God is high, and you will be obedient to His instructions. When the gift of faith comes on you, you are not the least bit concerned with what people will think about you.

There is coming a time where you may run across somebody like the lame man at the Gate Beautiful who doesn't know that God loves him or even cares what happens to him. Suddenly, the gift of faith will come on you, and you are going to see him miraculously set free.

When the gift of faith comes on you, you become very bold. When it lifts, you are just your regular self. There have been times early in my ministry where I was too afraid to say anything.

You have to guard against being timid. You don't ever want to back away from what God wants to do. The lives of many people can be dramatically changed if you will step out in faith. I am ready for that to start happening, aren't you?

Getting Immediate Results

In the mid-80s I was praying for a minister friend of mine who lives in Detroit, Michigan. As I was praying, I began to say things by the Spirit of God. All of a sudden the gift of faith came on me, and an angel appeared in the room. It scared me so bad that it felt as though the hair on the back of my head stood up!

When the angel walked into the room, he said, "I've been sent from the throne of God to tell you such and such," which was exactly what I had been praying about for that minister. Then, the angel gave me the answer to my prayer.

When I began to pray for the minister, I was not expecting an immediate answer. In fact, I thought the answer would come one of these days. But when the gift of faith came on me, the answer came immediately.

Always a Gentleman

The Holy Spirit will never push you to do anything. Don't think that you are being taken over by the Holy Spirit when the gift of faith manifests. I guarantee you that God won't knock you on the head to get you to operate in this gift. You have to yield to Him.

God won't ever intrude in your life. He will wait until you invite Him in. You don't do that to people you know, and God would not do that to you.

You would never knock on your neighbor's door and ask him how much money he has in his checkbook. He probably would close the door in your face if you did. You don't have any right to know how much money he has.

In the same way, the Holy Spirit does not have any right to operate in your life unless you give Him permission. He respects you that much.

The Apostle of Faith

Smith Wigglesworth is one of the best known modern-day examples of a person who operated in the gift of faith. While he was praying for a person, he could sense in his heart if that person was receiving or not.

If the person wasn't, the gift of faith would come on him. He would penetrate heaven with a faith that would not be denied, and the answer would come instantly.

As we approach the return of the Lord, I believe more people will begin to operate in the gift of faith. It will happen when people least expect it.

Peter and John were walking down the street when the Holy Spirit suddenly came on them. It's not recorded in any passage of Scripture that the Holy Spirit gave them a vision and told them what He planned on doing later that day.

The spirit of faith is so powerful that when it manifests, you won't have any doubt whether it was God or not. Your faith will rise to such a level that you will know that you know that this is God.

Raising People From the Dead

Smith Wigglesworth probably raised more people from the dead than anybody else. In one case, he was scheduled to preside over the memorial service of a deacon in his church. As the funeral was about to start, the ushers were getting ready to bring the casket to the front of the church.

The Holy Spirit spoke to Smith Wigglesworth and told him to raise the man from the dead. He pulled the lifeless body out of the casket and drug it down the center aisle.

Can you imagine the horror on the faces of the people in the church? He then sat the dead man on a chair and said, "Our brother has a testimony for us." The deacon immediately came to life and testified!

Three gifts of the Spirit need to be in operation to raise someone from the dead. It will take the gift of faith, the working of miracles, and the gifts of healings to get the job done.

You will need the gift of faith to call a spirit back, the working of miracles to get it back, and the gifts of healings to fix whatever it was that caused the person to die in the first place. If the gifts of healings don't manifest, the person will die again.

It's easy to know if the gift of faith is in operation. You have heard the saying, "The proof of the pudding is in the eating." If the dead person does not come back, you will know the gift of faith did not manifest!

The platform for special faith to operate is bold, ordinary faith. The bolder you are, the more the gift of faith will manifest in your life.

The only way to build your faith is to continually meditate on and confess the Word of God. Then, as your faith becomes stronger, you won't hesitate to do what God has told you to do.

Now is the time to step out in the things of God. Like the slogan in Nike ads, "Just do it." Let me assure you that

God will be there to manifest His goodness to those you are ministering to.

Romans 2:4 says that it is the goodness of God that brings men to repentance. Let's step out in the gifts of the Spirit so people can see how good God really is.

Chapter Ten

Combating Sickness and Disease

$\mathcal{E}$veryone is a minister although not everyone is in the five-fold ministry and makes a living from the ministry. Just because you are not in the full-time ministry, does not mean that the gifts of the Spirit cannot work through you in a big way.

Stephen is a good example of somebody who was in the ministry of helps and who *"...did great wonders and miracles among the people"* (Acts 6:8).

The early church began to experience persecution shortly after the day of Pentecost. Because they were so full of the Holy Spirit, they were undeterred by the persecution that came on them. Even after the death of Stephen, they continued preaching the Gospel.

The persecution did scatter the believers everywhere. (Acts 8:1-4.) However, they did not go into hiding when they fled Jerusalem; they continued to preach the Word wherever they were.

Like the early church, the end-time church can expect persecution when the gifts of the Spirit begin to manifest. If it happened then, you can count on it happening today.

We can also see from what happened to the early church where our persecution will come from. The church's main antagonists weren't the sinners. Their persecution came from the religious community.

When Stephen stood before his accusers, he said to the high priest, *"Ye stiffnecked and uncircumcised in heart and ears, ye do always resist the Holy Ghost..."* (Acts 7:51).

We also see from this scripture that the early church was not persecuted for preaching the Word of God. They were persecuted because the gifts of the Spirit manifested when they preached the Word.

The Ministry of Reconciliation

If there ever was a time to pick up where the early church left off, now is that time. We need to be preaching the message of reconciliation, with signs following everywhere.

Here is another example of the Holy Spirit working mightily through Philip.

> *Then Philip went down to the city of Samaria, and preached Christ unto them. And the people with one accord gave heed unto those things which Philip spake, hearing*

and seeing the miracles which he did. For unclean spirits,
crying with loud voice, came out of many that were
possessed with them: and many taken with palsies, and that
were lame, were healed.

ACTS 8:5-7

Philip was busy doing the Father's business; and as a
result, many miracles were performed. You will notice that
many, but not *everybody,* got healed.

While Jesus healed every manner of sickness and
disease (Matt. 4:23), we don't have record of any blind or
deaf people getting healed in Philip's ministry. That does
not mean it wasn't God's will for them to be healed; it just
means that the gifts of healings Philip operated in dealt
with people who were paralyzed and who were lame. These
were the tools God gave him to complete his calling.

Spreading the Gospel Through Healing

It's a good thing the church became scattered. The
presence and power of God that dwelt in the believers also
became scattered. If the believers had stayed in Jerusalem,
their ministry would have been limited to that city.

In John 14:12, Jesus said that we would do greater
works than He did. By that He meant that we would do a
greater number of works than He did.

He was just one man and was limited in what He could do. When Jesus walked the earth, you had to be where He was to get healed. He multiplied Himself when He gave the 12 disciples the power to lay hands on the sick. (Luke 9:1,2.) He later sent 70 men out. (Luke 10:1.)

When He ascended into heaven, He commissioned the entire church to preach to the captives. (Mark 16:15.) As part of our commission, we should expect the gifts of healings to be in operation.

The definition of the *gifts of healings* is "the gift or manifestation to deliver the sick and to destroy the works of the devil in the human body."

The gifts of healings should not be confused with *natural* healing received through medical science. It is being divinely healed by God.

I thank God for doctors. They are against sickness and disease, sometimes more than some religious folks are. Although they can do some marvelous things, like separate conjoined twins and transplant organs, what they do is not supernatural.

Specific Areas of Healing

After I graduated from Rhema in 1981, a pattern of healings began to develop in my ministry. People with growths, lumps, and injuries were healed time and again.

God gave me these giftings as tools for ministry. They don't belong to me. If they did, I would find every person who is troubled in these areas and say, "I have a gift for you." I would lay hands on them and watch them get healed.

Howard Carter was a minister from England who was born in 1891. He had a ministry of getting people filled with the Holy Spirit. Anybody he laid hands on to be baptized in the Holy Spirit instantly received.

If somebody needed prayer for healing, he would send them to his wife, as this was her area of ministry. He would tell them, "I can lay hands on you to be healed, but why don't you let my wife pray for you. She is gifted in that area and has a much better rate of success than I do."

As you begin to step out in laying hands on the sick, you will notice the same thing happen in your life. People with certain ailments will always get healed.

As each member of the body of Christ operates in the gift that was given to him or her, we will see 100 percent of the manifestations that operated in Jesus' ministry while He was on the earth.

A Vision of Healing

One time I was sitting on the front row in a service. The pastor had finished his sermon and called people up for prayer. Before he began laying hands on the people, he paused for a moment and said, "I'm going to have Brother Joe come up. He has been used in this area more than I have."

At that moment, I received a word of knowledge in the form of a vision. I saw an x-ray of woman's head. I walked up to a lady in the line. I knew in my heart that the x-ray I saw was of her head.

"You have something wrong with your head, don't you?" I asked.

"I sure do," she said.

"I just saw an x-ray, and I saw a spot about the size of a fist in your brain. Is that right?"

"That's right," she said. "I'm going for another x-ray tomorrow."

I said, "Praise God! God is going to heal you. I saw it just a minute ago as I sat on the front row." When I laid hands on her, I did not feel anything special. I did not have any goose bumps or see any angels.

The lady did not get real excited, but she was healed that night. The pastor later called me and told me that when she went in the next day for x-rays, the spot was gone!

The Working of Miracles

The early church believed in the power of God. They never believed that God was a weak God. They knew that He was all-powerful, and they demonstrated that power everywhere they went.

They easily moved from one gift to another. This is evidenced by the extensive instruction Paul gave the church of Corinth. (1 Cor. 14.) Everyone came to church ready to move in the Spirit, but instead of the people being edified, it was utter chaos.

Today, however, many people think it is easier to step out in giving a tongue and interpretation of tongues than it is to step out in the other gifts of the Spirit.

I want you to look at the following verses. You will see that the operation of one gift doesn't differ from another.

For to one is given by the Spirit the word of wisdom; to another the word of knowledge by the same Spirit; To another faith by the same Spirit; to another the gifts of healings by the same Spirit; To another the working of miracles; to another prophecy; to another discerning of spirits; to another divers kinds of tongues; to another the interpretation of tongues.

1 CORINTHIANS 12:8-10

Do you notice how many times "by the same Spirit" is repeated? It seems as though God is trying to get something through to us.

The same Holy Spirit who will give you a tongue and interpretation of tongues will also give you the working of miracles, the gifts of healings, and the gift of special faith. If you learn how to yield to Him in tongues and interpretation of tongues, you yield to the Holy Spirit in the working of miracles and the gifts of healings in the same way.

The working of miracles displays God's power and magnificence. The word *miracles* comes from the Greek word *dunamis,* which can be translated as "power."

In the Greek, they called this gift the working of power. In the *Young's Analytical Concordance, dunamis* is defined as "explosions of mightiness." You could define the working of miracles as the "working of the explosions of the mightiness of God."

Here are some examples of the working of miracles found in the Old Testament.

Miracles Manifested Through the Prophets

Elijah operated in the working of miracles when he twice called fire down from heaven in 2 Kings 1:10-12. He wanted the people to see that this miracle was not performed by his hand but by the power of God, so he said, *"If I be a man of God, let fire come down from heaven, and consume thee and thy fifty. And the fire of God came down from heaven, and consumed him and his fifty"* (v. 10).

After Elijah was taken to heaven in a chariot, his mantel fell to the earth. Elisha picked it up and went to the bank of Jordan River. He struck the river with the mantel, and the waters parted. (2 Kings 2:14.)

The difference between the gift of special faith and the working of miracles is that the gift of special faith is passive; it *receives* a miracle. The working of miracles, on the other hand, *does* a miracle. Elisha didn't *receive* the miracle of the river parting, he *did* it.

New Testament Examples

The working of miracles was demonstrated in Jesus' life on several occasions. The first miracle He ever performed was a working of miracles when He turned water into wine at a wedding reception. (John 2:1-11.)

He walked on the water. I find it amusing that when He decided to trek out across the lake, it was during a violent storm. Like walking across a calm body of water would have been easier and less miraculous! (Matt. 14:24-26; John 6:18,19.)

He also raised two people from the dead. In Luke 7:12-15, He was moved with compassion when He saw a widow woman weeping over her dead son and raised him from the dead. Most everyone is familiar with the story of Lazarus in John 11.

What is interesting about Lazarus' situation is that when Jesus first heard that he was gravely ill, He stayed where He was for two more days. (John 11:6.) When He finally arrived at the home of Mary and Martha, He quickly raised their brother from the grave.

If Jesus did these things while He was here on the earth, the church should be doing these same things while He is in heaven. Jesus does not want us to shrink back from the miraculous. He wants us to boldly allow His power to flow through us so that miracles become a normal part of our lives.

Here is another example of the working of miracles that involves the apostles. After Jesus had ascended into heaven, the apostles were busy preaching the Gospel in Jerusalem. The religious people of their day became indignant with their message and had all of apostles put in prison. An angel of the Lord came in the middle of the night and opened the prison doors and told them to go back to the Temple and continue preaching the Word. (Acts 5:16-23.)

That is the best way to break out of jail—have an angel show up and open all of the doors. We don't see that they prayed and asked God for their deliverance. They were so busy doing the works of Jesus that God couldn't afford to have them locked up in jail. So He sent an angel to break them out!

Restoring Body Parts

It's through the working of miracles that missing body parts are restored. If you somehow lost an arm or a leg, either due to sickness or through an accident, God cannot heal something that is not there. But He can restore what you once had or what should be there.

We have something better than any of the gifts of the Spirit and that is the Word of God. When Jesus died on the Cross, He not only bore your sins, but He also obtained healing for your body. You can stand on God's healing Word for anything and be healed and restored without anyone laying hands on you. The Word will work if you will keep holding on to it.

Judgment in the Early Church

In addition to the wonderful miracles that were just mentioned, the working of miracles was sometimes used in

the form of judgment. An example of this is found in the book of Acts.

The people in the early church were moved by the Spirit of God to sell their possessions and give the money to the church. Here is what happened to one couple whose hearts were not right before God.

> *But a certain man named Ananias, with Sapphira his wife, sold a possession, And kept back part of the price, his wife also being privy to it, and brought a certain part, and laid it at the apostles' feet. But Peter said, Ananias, why hath Satan filled thine heart to lie to the Holy Ghost, and to keep back part of the price of the land? Whiles it remained, was it not thine own? and after it was sold, was it not in thine own power? why hast thou conceived this thing in thine heart? thou hast not lied unto men, but unto God.*

ACTS 5:1-4

Peter could not have known this information on his own; he received a word of knowledge of what Ananias and his wife had conspired to do. Notice that Peter said they could have kept back part of the proceeds of the sale of the land if they had wanted to. Instead, they lied. They thought they would look better in the sight of others if they said they had given everything.

When Ananias heard Peter's words, he died instantly. The church's youth group was given the task of burying him. I cannot think of a better way to teach young people to reverence God than to have somebody drop dead in church.

I can imagine a young man dragging Ananias outside and asking, "How did he die?" "He lied." That will strike fear in the hearts of people.

If this had happened today, half of the church would have been on their cell phones calling his wife and everybody else they knew. But no one in the early church told Ananias' wife anything. They were probably too afraid to talk to her.

Three hours later, Sapphira came back, and Peter asked her the same questions. She gave the same answers that Ananias did.

Peter said in verse 9, *"How is it that ye have agreed together to tempt the Spirit of the Lord?"* She also died the same way her husband did.

Isn't it amazing that they thought they could hide what they were doing from God? We often think that nobody will know what we do behind closed doors, but that's not true. The Holy Spirit knows everybody's secrets.

Judgment Today

In the last days, people will still try to lie to the Holy Spirit, and they won't be able to get away with it. Now is not the time to come against the things of God. It won't work. I fear for anyone who tries. We are going to see more incidents like Ananias and Sapphira.

Fifteen years ago, you might have been able to get away with secret sin but not anymore. The closer we get to the return of the Lord, the more critical it will be for God to accomplish His will on the earth.

God's mercy has been long suffering for a very long time, but His patience is about to run out. Anything that will hinder the move of God will have to be moved out of the way.

The deaths of Ananias and Sapphira shook up the entire community. The Scripture says that nobody else would join the early church even though they held the people in high esteem. (v. 13.) Their deaths got the church's attention. You better believe that everyone who had joined him- or herself to the apostles lived a sin-free life.

Many times people say that they couldn't help themselves when they sinned. I can assure you that if people start dropping dead in church, people will suddenly be able to get their flesh under control.

Their deaths didn't stop the move of God. Miracles continued to happen, and people kept giving their hearts to Christ. We see in verse 15 that *"they brought forth the sick into the streets, and laid them on beds and couches, that at the least the shadow of Peter passing by might overshadow some of them."*

We need to believe that things like this will happen today. Can you imagine if people who were in stretchers and wheelchairs lined up on the sidewalk so when the minister was entering the church building, his or her shadow might fall on them?

God is not a respecter of persons. Just because we have an example of this in the Bible, means that we can expect it to happen for us today.

Blinded for a Season

Another example of judgment is found in Acts 13. The church had been fasting and praying when the Holy Spirit separated Barnabus and Paul from the rest of the company for the work that they had been called to. After hands had been laid on them, they set sail for Cyprus.

From there they traveled through the surrounding islands until they came to Paphos. On the Isle of Paphos, they encountered a sorcerer who opposed the work they were doing. The Spirit of the Lord came upon Paul, and he fastened his eyes on the sorcerer and said,

O full of all subtilty and all mischief, thou child of the devil, thou enemy of all righteousness, wilt thou not cease to pervert the right ways of the Lord? And now, behold, the hand of the Lord is upon thee, and thou shalt be blind, not seeing the sun for a season. And immediately there fell on

*him a mist and a darkness; and he went about seeking
some to lead him by the hand.*

ACTS 13:10,11

This false prophet wanted to keep people from hearing
the Gospel by trying to *"pervert the right ways of the Lord."* As
Paul and Barnabus were preaching, he was going behind
their backs trying to pervert the Gospel.

God didn't like what he was doing, so he struck the
sorcerer blind for a season. That will teach you to mess
with the things of God!

Doing the Lord's Work

The Holy Spirit wants everybody to get healed, and He
will use every single one of us if we will be open to His
leadings. We have to get out of the mindset that we can
only be used in tongues and interpretation of tongues.

I hear the sound of the abundance of rain. I hear the
wind of God that is flowing through the church. God is
pouring His power out on people who are ready to
receive it.

If I had a pitcher of water and you told me you wanted
some water, do you think I would start pouring the water if
you didn't have a glass? No. I would not give you anything
until you were ready to receive it. It is the same with the
gifts of the Spirit.

God will pour out His Spirit on the people who are ready to walk in the things of God. People have said, "I've heard about this all my life. I wonder if we are ever going to see it happen."

We are on the verge of seeing the greatest miracles happen that we have ever dreamed of. Don't cast away your confidence. Jesus said, "If you believe you will see." (Mark 9:23.)

Chapter Eleven

God's Mouthpiece

$\mathcal{M}$ost people believe that God will equip the five-fold ministry gifts—apostles, prophets, evangelists, pastors, and teachers—with the necessary tools to fulfill their calls. But these same people do not believe that God meant for the gifts of the Spirit to operate through them.

While they may go so far as to prophesy or give a tongues and an interpretation of tongues, they believe that receiving a word of wisdom or operating in the working of miracles is beyond their reach. I believe, however, that in the last days God is going to pour out His Spirit on *all* flesh and will use anyone who makes him- or herself available.

The Gift of Prophecy

The vocal gifts have been abused more than any of the other gifts of the Spirit. The reason is that people have a part to play in what is being said.

God does not take over your mind and body and turn you into another person when you prophesy or give a tongues and interpretation of tongues. You are in full control of your faculties when you speak, and that is why errors can occur.

Sometimes people are afraid to step out in giving a prophecy. When they do, they may stumble over their words and then try to make up for their tied tongue by trying to say something that sounds spiritual.

Many times they pray for a special touch from God before they speak. They want some type of assurance that it is really God who is prodding their hearts to prophesy. This usually never happens.

A lot of times, you will only receive a single word to say. You must take a step of faith and speak that one word, believing that the rest of the prophecy will follow. Everything in Christianity is based on faith. If God made everything crystal clear for us, we wouldn't be walking by faith.

The definition for *prophecy* is a "supernatural utterance in a known tongue." It also means "to flow forth" and carries with it the thought "to bubble forth like a fountain; and to lift up." As you spend time with the Lord, you can get so full of God that you feel like He is going to flow right through you.

Prophesy means "to speak for another; to speak for God, as to be His spokesman." We are God's mouth-pieces on the earth today. If we do not yield to prophecy, what He wants to say regarding this day and hour will not get said.

There is a difference between the simple gift of prophecy and prophecy that includes the word of wisdom. Simple prophecy edifies, comforts, and exhorts and does not include information about the future. If it does, it is really a word of wisdom and not prophecy.

Prophecy is not preaching. While a minister's message may be divinely inspired, the message is never considered a prophecy. A minister may prophesy while he or she is preaching, but the two are completely different.

Prophecy is more common than you may realize. It does not always have to be "Thus sayeth the Lord…." Some people have prophesied and didn't even know it.

Have you ever witnessed to somebody and things began to flow out of you that you did not know you knew? This is a form of prophecy. It may have felt like rivers of living water were gushing out of you as you ministered to uplift and edify that individual. This is a form of supernatural utterance.

Judging Prophecy

The apostle John instructs us to try the spirits to see whether or not they are of God. (1 John 4:1.) That shows me that there are going to be some spirits that are not of God. How can you tell by which spirit a person is operating?

There are three ways that you can judge the prophecy you hear and know whether or not it is from God. First, prophecy will always edify, exhort, and comfort. Paul said in 1 Corinthians 14:3, *"he that prophesieth speaketh unto men to edification, and exhortation, and comfort."*

The word *edify* means "to charge up." After hearing a prophecy, you should be charged up. The word *exhort* means "to call near to God." Prophecy should cause you to have more of a reverence for God, not less. You should feel like you just got finished talking with the Lord after hearing a prophecy.

Next, prophecy will glorify God and magnify what Jesus did on the Cross 2,000 years ago. It should draw your attention to Jesus and not to the person giving it. If it magnifies the individual, then you can know with assurance that God is not in what that person is saying.

Finally, prophecy will always be in line with the written Word of God. Anything that God says verbally will not contradict what He has already written in His Word. If somebody prophesies that God puts sickness on you to

teach you a lesson, you can immediately know that it is not from God.

John 10:10 says, *"The thief cometh not, but for to steal, and to kill, and to destroy: I am come that they might have life, and that they might have it more abundantly."* And 1 Peter 2:24 says, *"Who his own self bare our sins in his own body on the tree, that we, being dead to sins, should live unto righteousness: by whose stripes ye were healed."*

This is a good example of why it is important to know the Word. If you did not know these Scriptures, you might believe a false prophecy. As soon as you hear something that contradicts God's Word, you know to immediately throw it out.

Peter said that we have a more sure word of prophecy. (2 Peter 1:19.) In other words, you never have to seek after a verbal word from God above the written Word. The written Word contains every answer you will need for any situation you encounter.

I am convinced that we are going to see many false prophets in the last days. It will look as though they are being used by the Holy Spirit, but they will actually be operating through a false spirit. If you follow the above steps, you will always be able to discern whether or not they are of God.

Yielding to the Vocal Gifts

The vocal gifts were meant to inspire the body of Christ and keep us full of God so that we can be ready when God wants to manifest the other gifts.

I like the power gifts. If it were up to me, I would operate in the gifts of healings all the time. I like to see people's bodies restored and made whole.

However, the Lord told me one time that the body of Christ will never learn how to flow in the revelation and the power gifts until they learn how to yield to the vocal gifts. Most people find it easier to yield to the vocal gifts.

You can be certain that if you won't yield to the Lord when He wants you to prophesy, you won't yield to Him when He wants to use you in the working of miracles either. We have to learn to how respond to prophecy before we can learn how to respond to the word of wisdom or the gift of special faith.

Another thing to keep in mind is that prophecy is not meant to always be given inside the church building. You ought to be prophesying in your home or anywhere you may be when God wants to speak.

There have been many times when I have been praying for somebody in tongues, and the Lord gave me words in English to pray over that person. That's prophecy. You can also be in a restaurant or driving with somebody in your

car when God has a word for them. The more you yield to the Spirit in times like this, the easier it will be to prophesy when you are in church.

Decently and In Order

Paul wrote chapters 12 through 14 in 1 Corinthians to give the Corinthian church instruction on how to establish order in their church services. The members of this church were not timid in operating in the gifts.

They were so full of the Holy Spirit that they all wanted to prophesy and minister in the gifts of the Spirit. Unfortunately, it was usually at the same time.

First Corinthians 14:26 says, *"How is it then, brethren? when ye come together, every one of you hath a psalm, hath a doctrine, hath a tongue, hath a revelation, hath an interpretation. Let all things be done unto edifying."*

We need to get back to this today. The Corinthians came to church ready to give. Today, some people come to church so empty that it can be halfway through the service before they start to receive.

Even though the Corinthian church services were somewhat chaotic, I think it is better to have a little wild-fire in a service than no fire at all. It's easier to guide people in the proper use of the gifts than it is to strike a fire under their feet.

Paul had to reign in the excitement the Corinthians had in flowing in the gifts of the Spirit. God wants every person who comes to a service to be edified. He wants to make sure that everybody understands what is going on when the Spirit is moving. When there is confusion and things are done out of order, nobody is edified.

One time I was in a meeting, and a lady began to prophesy. I immediately knew it was a wrong spirit, because what she was saying didn't line up with the Bible. In the middle of her prophecy, the fan for the air conditioning unit kicked on, and you could not hear a word she had said. I thought, *Now that's a sign from God!*

When you first begin to prophesy, you may miss it a couple of times before you get it right. If you stumble when you speak, don't afterward say, "I am never going to do that again." We all make mistakes. You will become proficient in prophesying as you continue to step out when the Lord prompts you to give a word.

When I was a kid, I fell a lot when I was learning how to ride a bicycle. I had plenty of cuts and bruises to show for all my efforts. I kept getting up and trying again until eventually I could ride a bike effortlessly.

It's the same with the things of God. We are never going to be perfect the first time we step out. God may only want you to say two words. He might not want you to talk for 30 minutes. Sometimes we miss it because we try to "fill

in" for God. But really, we are just trying to be spiritual when we're not.

Personal Prophecy

Another type of prophecy is personal prophecy. Although personal prophecy is scriptural, I must give a word of caution along with it. If somebody prophesies to you, it should confirm what God has already spoken to your heart.

If you are hearing something for the first time, then my advice is to either throw it out or put it on a shelf. Time will tell if it was from God.

If somebody prophecies that you are supposed to marry a particular individual or that you are supposed to give a certain amount of money in the offering, throw it out. This type of prophecy is not from God. He won't force you to marry anybody—especially if you think the person is ugly!

Second Corinthians 9:7 instructs you to give what you have purposed in your heart. God will speak to you about what you should give. He won't use someone to prophesy to you the amount of money you should give in an offering. Prophecies like these are only forms of manipulation on the part of the one who is giving them.

A biblical example of personal prophecy is found in Acts 13:2. *"As they ministered to the Lord, and fasted, the Holy*

Ghost said, Separate me Barnabas and Saul for the work where-unto I have called them."

Notice the atmosphere that enabled the Holy Spirit to manifest. They were fasting and ministering to the Lord. This opened the door for prophecy to come forth. You will notice that this prophecy *confirmed* the call of God on Paul's and Barnabus's lives. They were not hearing it for the first time.

People have backed away from prophecy because it has been abused. Too many personal prophecies have been given that have been way off track, and people's lives have been hurt.

Just because something has been abused, does not mean that we throw out all prophecy. We see in this verse how personal prophecy was beneficial to what Paul and Barnabus were called to do.

I have had people tell me things that bore witness to what was on the inside of my heart. The Lord had already dealt with me about it several times before.

One time I was praying about an upcoming service. The Lord showed me what He wanted me to do in the service, but I didn't want to do it and argued with Him. I felt that it would take too much time to do things His way. As I continued to pray, I finally said, "All right, Lord. I'll do it. If that is what You want me to do, I will do it."

In the service the next day, I was at the book table when a little old Pentecostal lady came up to me. I could see that the Spirit of the Lord was coming on her. She grabbed my hand and prophesied to me exactly what the Lord had told me that night before. Boy did she read my mail! Even though I had reluctantly given in to the Lord, she confirmed everything that God had said to me.

We are not to be led by prophecy. It should only confirm what is already in your heart. The first ten years of my ministry I never received a personal prophecy. If you never receive one either, that's okay. You have the written Word as well as your inward witness to lead and guide you.

Romans 14:19 says, *"Let us therefore follow after the things which make for peace...."* Colossians 3:15 also says, *"And let the peace of God rule in your hearts...."* Peace is always a good guide to follow when making a decision.

The Office of a Prophet

One of the biggest bandwagons I have seen in the body of Christ is the number of people who call themselves prophets. Just because you put the title in front of your name does not make you a prophet or any of the other five-fold ministry gifts.

Likewise, just because you have prophesied a time or two does not make you a prophet. To be in the office of prophet, in addition to prophesying, all three of the revelation gifts need to consistently operate in your life.

I think some people believe they are prophets because they had a word of knowledge about somebody one time. They then broadcast to anyone who will listen that they stand in this office.

Proverbs 18:6 says that your gift will make room for you. True prophets don't have to publicize their ministries. It will be evident to everyone around you what office you do or don't stand in.

In Acts 21 the prophet Agabus had four daughters who prophesied. (v. 9.) The Scripture doesn't say that his daughters were prophets; they only prophesied.

Only Agabus is recorded as being a prophet. In verse 11 he foretold what was going to happen to Paul when he went to Jerusalem. Since he told Paul of future events that would happen to him, he really gave him a word of wisdom rather than prophesied to him.

While everyone should be able to operate in the simple gift of prophecy, not many people will receive a special manifestation of prophecy that includes the word of wisdom or word of knowledge.

Be Full of the Holy Spirit

When the angel Gabriel appeared to Mary to tell her that she would become pregnant with the Christ, he also told her that her cousin Elizabeth was pregnant. When Mary later visited Elizabeth at her home, Elizabeth's baby leapt inside her womb at Mary's salutation. The Scripture says that Elizabeth was filled with the Holy Spirit and began to prophesy. (Luke 1:41,42.)

The account of John the Baptist's birth is also recorded in Luke 1. You will remember that Zechariah had not been able to speak a word since the angel Gabriel visited him to tell him that his barren wife would bare a child.

After the baby was born, family members wanted to name the child Zechariah, after his father. When Zechariah wrote on a tablet that the child's name was to be John, his mouth was loosed. (Luke 1:64.)

He also became filled with the Holy Spirit and began to prophesy. (v. 67.) There is no record that Elizabeth or Zechariah had ever prophesied before or after these incidents and neither were they ever considered to be prophets.

Acts 2:18 says, *"And on my servants and on my handmaidens I will pour out in those days of my Spirit; and they shall prophesy."* This is what happened to Elizabeth and Zechariah. When they became full of the Holy Spirit, prophecy bubbled forth out of both of them.

To become full of the Holy Spirit, feed on the Word of God and pray in tongues. Praying in tongues will make your inner man sensitive to the leadings of the Holy Spirit, and meditating on Scripture will cause the Word of God to come out of your mouth when you prophesy.

The more you hook your tongue up with a heart full of the Word, the fuller you are and the more ready you will be when the Holy Spirit comes on you.

We are instructed not to be drunk with wine, but instead to be full of the Holy Spirit. (Eph. 5:18.) What is the connection with being drunk and being filled with the Spirit?

I'm sure you have seen somebody who was drunk, either in real life or in the movies. Did you notice that they say whatever is on their mind? They will spill their guts to anybody. They don't care who they are talking to. Somebody they know or a perfect stranger. They don't have any inhibitions.

Likewise, when you are full of the Holy Spirit, you won't have any inhibitions speaking out for God. When the Holy Spirit gives you the unction to prophesy, you will boldly proclaim what God wants to say and all those around you will be blessed.

Chapter Twelve

Interpreting Mysteries

I once heard a story about a preacher in Oregon who ministered each week on live TV. On one occasion in the middle of his message, he began to speak in tongues. However, after he gave the tongue, he did not receive an interpretation.

He was well aware that 1 Corinthians 14:13 says, *"let him that speaketh in an unknown tongue pray that he may interpret."* He prayed for an interpretation but nothing came. He did not know what to do, so he just stood there. Eventually, he stumbled through the remainder of his sermon before going off the air.

You can imagine his relief when a woman later called his ministry to tell him what had happened to her as she was watching the broadcast. This woman lived in Germany most of her life and spoke fluent German.

She had been watching the minister's broadcast but then got busy doing other things. When he spoke in tongues during the television program, he spoke in a dialect that was only spoken in one part of Germany.

He said in the uncommon dialect, "Woman...." This caught her attention, so she stopped what she was doing and looked at the TV. "Yes, that's right," he continued. "Woman, I'm talking to you!" He then gave her the plan of salvation in her native tongue!

Grabbing Someone's Attention

The Great Commission in Mark 16:15 and 17 tells us to,

Go ye into all the world, and preach the gospel to every creature...And these signs shall follow them that believe; In my name shall they cast out devils; they shall speak with new tongues.

One of the signs that will follow believers is divers kinds of tongues. First Corinthians 14:22 says, *"Wherefore tongues are for a sign, not to them that believe, but to them that believe not...."* I believe that before the coming of the Lord, tongues will be used a lot more to get the unbeliever's attention, similar to what happened with the German lady in Oregon.

Here is another example of an unusual manifestation of divers tongues. I have a minister friend who is constantly traveling to countries around the world. After arriving in the different nations, however, he has never needed an interpreter. It's not that he is fluent in that many languages; he simply begins speaking in tongues, and the people understand him in their native languages.

What exactly is this unusual manifestation of the Spirit that has been given to believers around the world? *Divers kinds of tongues* is a "supernatural utterance of the Holy Spirit in a language never learned or understood by the speaker and not necessarily understood by the hearer." *Divers* means "different," or different kinds of tongues.

Hearing in Their Native Tongues

Even though the two examples I gave you are not common, they are biblical. On the day of Pentecost, the apostles and the 120 in the upper room were filled with the Holy Spirit and spoke with other tongues.

Jerusalem was filled with Jews from every nation, celebrating the Feast of Weeks or Shavuot. On this holiday, Jewish farmers brought their first fruit offerings to the Temple in Jerusalem thanking God for His hand in providing them with a bountiful harvest.

Like the two examples I gave you, the Jews on the day of Pentecost did not need an interpretation of what was said. Each person heard the apostles speak in his or her native language. (Acts 2:7-11.) Tongues got their attention

and opened the door for the Gospel to be preached, result-
ing in the salvation of 3,000 people.

The early church was birthed on the day of Pentecost,
a day associated with harvest and the bringing of first fruits
offerings to the Temple. I believe the Holy Spirit came on
this day so we would realize that we received the Holy
Spirit for one reason—to bring in the harvest.

I once asked the Lord what the end-time harvest was
going to be like. He said, "In the old days, men harvested
with sickles. In the last days, combines will be used." When
sickles were used, it took a long time to harvest a field.
Today, farmers can do more work in a shorter amount of
time by using combines.

The same will happen in the spirit realm. God is going
to do more in less time. I believe more souls will be
brought into the kingdom of God today than at any other
period in history.

The "combine" that God will use is the gifts of the
Spirit. The gifts will grab people's attention and open their
hearts to the preaching of the Word.

Acting Foolishly

When I was a student at Rhema, I worked at a limou-
sine company. One day I thought I would "try out" divers
kinds of tongues on some of the foreign people I picked up.

Although my doctrine was off, my intentions were good. I thought that I might be able to get someone saved. I would wait until the customers were settled in the back seat, and then I would start blabbing to them in tongues.

After I started speaking in tongues to one couple, they shook their heads and shrugged their shoulders. I realized that they didn't understand what I was saying, so I tried a different dialect in tongues.

Again they shook their heads. I just kept at it. I figured that sooner or later I would hit on a tongue they understood. I think they were actually impressed with the number of languages they thought I could speak. They did not know I was just plain stupid!

I was trying to operate the gifts of the Spirit rather than allowing the Holy Spirit to manifest Himself through me. Don't be like me and do this. Wait until you get an unction from the Holy Spirit.

The Interpretation of Tongues

After accepting Jesus as your Lord and Savior, the next step is to be baptized in the Holy Spirit with the evidence of speaking in tongues. After you receive your prayer language, you can speak in tongues at anytime and anyplace.

You don't have to have a feeling or a manifestation of the Holy Spirit to pray in tongues. You can be working around your house or driving in your car while praying.

Your prayer language is not the same as when the Holy Spirit comes on you to give you a word in tongues during a church service. Tongues and the interpretation of tongues working together equal prophecy.

When a tongue is given, the interpretation of tongues is needed to receive the full benefit of the tongue. The definition of *interpretation of tongues* is "the meaning of an utterance in other tongues."

God doesn't want any kind of confusion in a service. If you feel led to give a tongue but can't interpret and don't know if somebody in the service can, the Apostle Paul's instructions in 1 Corinthians 14:28 are to keep quiet and not to say anything. Why? The answer is found in verses four and five of that same chapter.

"He that speaketh in an unknown tongue edifieth himself; but he that prophesieth edifieth the church. I would that ye all spake with tongues but rather that ye prophesied: for greater is he that prophesieth than he that speaketh with tongues, except he interpret, that the church may receive edifying."

The couple in the back of the limo I drove did not understand one word I said. My babbling did not edify them or draw them any closer to the Lord.

I remember the first time I heard tongues and interpretation of tongues. I was just a little kid. Even though my brain thought it was pretty strange, something on the inside of me said, "Wow! That's God!"

You may have noticed that the length of a tongue and the length of the interpretation of the tongue are often different. A tongue can be extremely long and the interpretation very short, or vice versa. That's because the interpretation is just that, an interpretation, not a translation.

Like prophecy, tongues and interpretation of tongues will always be in line with the Word of God. If the interpretation of the tongue does not line up with the Word or glorify Jesus, then you know it's not of God. Don't give heed or pay any attention to it. Just throw it out.

Being Weird Instead of Spiritual

The 14th chapter of 1 Corinthians is an instruction manual on how to operate in the gifts of the Spirit when the church assembles together. Why all the regulations?

In 1 Corinthians 14:23 it says, *"If therefore the whole church be come together into one place, and all speak with tongues, and there come in those that are unlearned, or unbelievers, will they not say that ye are mad?"*

If unbelievers happen to be in the congregation and witness people randomly standing up and speaking in

foreign languages, they would not have any idea of what was going on. They probably would never come back. God wants everybody who comes to church to be edified, and this happens when the church services are conducted decently and in order.

God is not Mickey Mouse or weird. He is normal. He is so normal that I think it blows most of us away! I believe that He wants us to treat the vocal gifts as a normal part of our lives. That way we won't seek the gift but rather seek to be a blessing to those around us.

Christians can sometimes get so caught up in the Holy Spirit that they do weird things. When you talk to them later, they will tell you, "I just couldn't help it! I had to prophesy!"

That's not true. They are operating out of their emotions and will be a distraction in the service. First Corinthians 14:32 says, *"the spirits of the prophets are subject to the prophets."* In other words, you are in control of your spirit and are in subjection to yourself.

The Holy Spirit will never *force* you to do anything. The devil, however, will push you to do things in a service when you should not. If you ever feel "compelled" to interrupt a minister, it's probably not God.

If the Holy Spirit is flowing through the pastor or guest minister while he or she is preaching, He will never use someone in the congregation to interrupt Himself to get a point across.

The Holy Spirit is orderly. When He prompts you to do or say something, your obedience should not cause confusion in the service.

I was in a church in Colorado and had turned the service over to the pastor. He had prayed the benediction and was saying goodnight to everybody when someone in the balcony broke out in tongues. This man was out of order. Obviously, it was not the right time to speak.

Maybe the Holy Spirit had wanted the tongue to be spoken earlier in the service, but the man was too fearful to step out. When he missed his opportunity, he should have kept the tongue to himself instead of trying to give it when the congregation was walking out of the door.

Following the Pastor's Lead

Here are some simple housekeeping rules that you should always follow. God has set the pastor as the head over his or her church. Proper church order dictates that God speaks to the pastor about matters regarding that church.

While God will talk to you about your personal matters or how you should become involved in your church, He will never talk to you about how the church should be run or what the pastor should be doing. You have to trust the

pastor's sensitivity to hear the voice of the Holy Spirit and to be obedient to God in this area.

If your pastor has set procedures in place for how he wants the gifts of the Spirit to operate in his church, then you must follow those guidelines whether you agree with them or not. God has placed the pastor as the head over that body, not you.

Another important point to remember. If, when you step out in any of the manifestations of the Spirit, you miss it and your pastor has to correct you, don't get offended and leave the church. You need to be a grown up when it comes to the things of the Spirit.

Whenever you miss it, take the correction and go on. When parents have to discipline their children, normally the kids don't run away from home when they are punished. Learn from your mistake and be more careful not to do it again.

On the other hand, you may have felt the Holy Spirit prod at your heart to speak in tongues or to give a prophecy. Follow the guidelines your pastor has put in place and take a step of faith. Speak out what is in your heart.

If God won't "force" a person to become born again, He won't "force" you to yield to the Holy Spirit. He will never violate your will and "make" you say anything.

This is why the agony of hell will be so great. Everyone who is there chose to be there. However, if you continually ignore the promptings of the Holy Spirit, He will eventually stop tapping on your shoulder and move on to someone else.

In the last days, you will have many occasions to be used in the vocal gifts. I recommend that you take advantage of every opportunity that comes your way. Every time you yield to the Holy Spirit, you are making yourself more open to be used in mightier ways and for God to pour His power through you.

Orderly Worship

In 1 Corinthians 14:26-31 Paul gives extensive instructions on how to prophesy and give a tongues and interpretation of tongues. The Corinthian church services were too wild and chaotic, and he needed to bring order to the meetings.

If Christians at the service felt as though they were to give forth a tongue and interpretation of tongues, Paul instructed that only two, and at the most three, people give out a tongue. Those three people, then, could give out an unlimited number of tongues and interpretations during the service.

Prophecy is different. Any number of people can prophesy during a service. The reason Paul limits tongues

and interpretation of tongues is because this gift can be misunderstood if it's not used correctly.

Step Out and Be Used

I want to spur you into doing the things you know to do. If Christians would only operate in 5 percent of what they have been taught in church, we would see the miraculous happen all the time. We are coming into such an awesome move of God that the gifts of the Spirit operating through us must be an ordinary part of our lives.

We need to be so full of the power of God that people won't have to ask you what is different about you. They will know that God is all over you. Smith Wigglesworth was this way. People fell on their knees at his feet. They would grab his pant leg and cry, "You convict me of my sin. What must I do to be saved?"

We are coming to a time where that will happen to many of us. We need to stay full of the Holy Spirit so the power of God will do more than just flow *to* us, but instead flow *through* us to minister to others. Get ready for what God wants to do by being well versed in the gifts of the Spirit.

We are going to see people translated. I believe that as we get closer to the return of the Lord, we are going to see more of the glory of God become visible here on earth. We need to learn how to live in that glory so when we get raptured, we can be ushered into God's presence.

God wants us to be grounded in the Word so we are not weird when we operate in the gifts of the Spirit. He will then be able to use us in greater measures because we will direct the people's attention back to God.

Get ready for the final outpouring of the Spirit. The prophet Haggai said the glory of the latter house will be greater than the former. (Hag. 2:9.)

You want to be like the wise virgins who had their lanterns full of oil and were able to go into the wedding feast. The outpouring is just around the corner. You do not want it to pass you by.

Chapter Thirteen

Seeing Afar Off

$\mathcal{P}$eter encourages us to develop our faith by adding virtue along with a list of godly characteristics in 2 Peter 1:5-7. He goes on to say in verse 8, *"For if these things be in you, and abound, they make you that ye shall neither be barren nor unfruitful...."*

The word *barren* means "to be idle." God does not want us to be idle. He wants us to be witnessing whenever we have an opportunity, laying hands on the sick, and operating in the gifts of the Spirit.

As we do these things, we will add much fruit to our account. While we cannot bear fruit in and of ourselves, we see in John 15:4 that as we abide in Christ, we will be able to reap a harvest and see results that will be pleasing to God.

Unfortunately, many people in the church today are barren and unfruitful. They have not taken on the attitude of a servant and have been idle in doing the things of God.

When you are not bearing fruit, Peter says that you are
"...blind, and cannot see afar off..." (2 Peter 1:9).

Building for Eternity

When you look beyond the few short years that you
will be here, your attitude on how you live will change.
You will become more aggressive in the things of God,
because you know that your time on earth is just a vapor.
We only have a limited amount of time before Jesus
returns. What are you doing with the time you have left?

Are you eternity-minded, or are you focused on the
here and now? The Apostle Paul tells us to *"set [our] affec-
tion on things above, not on things on the earth"* (Col. 3:2). Many
people do not realize that what they do on the earth builds
for their eternity.

Everything you do in this life writes your résumé for
the next age. What does your eternal résumé have on it? Is
it blank, or is it filled with the exploits that you have done
for God?

Many Christians start out on fire for God, but something happens after they have been saved for a while.
They lose the zealousness they had when they first
became born again. Their initial excitement of escaping
hell has faded, and they have become content with sitting
back and relaxing.

Peter warns us not to let this happen. He says to *"...give diligence to make your calling and election sure..."* (2 Peter 1:10).

I have been far from perfect in my walk with the Lord, but at least I have endeavored to accomplish what He has asked me to do. When I stand before Him, I want to hear, "Well done, thou good and faithful servant." I don't want Him to say, "Joe, you were so clueless when you were on the earth."

Fighting the Fight of Faith

In the Word of Faith circles, we have been taught not to be "works" minded. We know that works won't get us into heaven. It is only by grace that you are saved through faith in Jesus Christ. (Eph. 2:8,9.) Only then is your name written in the Lamb's Book of Life. You can bake pies and do nice things for others, but your good deeds won't "buy" your way into heaven.

However, Christians have been taught against works for such a long time that now nobody wants to do anything for God. Many people think that they can sit on a church pew, soak up the Word, and still have the abundant entrance into heaven that Peter speaks of in 2 Peter 1:11. You can't. It won't work.

I know some people who have barely squeaked into heaven. Thank God for squeaking in; at least they're there. But it does not have to be that way.

I am writing my résumé with eternity in mind. I am doing whatever it takes now so that I can build for eternity. The Lord has a course that He wants all of us to finish. He wants us to trim the fat so we can finish the race that He has laid out for us. Paul said to Timothy,

> *...exercise thyself rather unto godliness. For bodily exercise profiteth little: but godliness is profitable unto all things, having promise of the life that now is, and of that which is to come.*

1 TIMOTHY 4:7,8

While bodily exercise is profitable for a short time, godliness is profitable for eternity. Godly living will not only pay off in our present life, but it will also last for eternity.

Paul later charged Timothy to *"fight the good fight of faith, lay hold on eternal life..."* (1 Tim. 6:12). The fact that He told Timothy to lay hold of eternal life indicates that you can live selfishly and only be concerned about what is happening in the here and now. Eternity can be far from your daily thoughts.

Things That Last for Eternity

What are some of the things that you can do to build an eternal treasure? Paul gives us some advice on how to do this.

> *Now if any man build upon this foundation gold, silver, precious stones, wood, hay, stubble; Every man's work shall be made manifest: for the day shall declare it, because it shall be revealed by fire; and the fire shall try every man's work of what sort it is.*

> 1 Corinthians 3:12,13

At the judgment seat of Christ, Christians will not be judged for sin. They will be judged for what they have done on earth. Their deeds will be tried by fire. The things that you have done that are made of gold, silver, and precious stones will be able to withstand the fire. But works that are made up of wood, hay, and stubble will be burned.

What types of things are wood, hay, and stubble? These are things that do not last a long time. You find wood, hay, and stubble above ground. These are the things you do so you can be seen of men.

When Jesus talked about the scribes and Pharisees in Matthew 23, He said, *"All their works they do for to be seen of men..."* (v. 5). They prayed loudly and sat in the best seats

in the synagogues. They received their reward on earth. These things, however, do not last for eternity.

Gold, silver, and precious stones are located below the earth. You have to dig to find them. One activity that is made up of gold is your devotional life. How much time do you spend in fellowship with the Lord every day? How often do you tell Him that you love Him?

There is a book of remembrance in heaven that contains all of the times you talk about the Lord. (Mal. 3:16.) Will your words be recorded in this book? What do you talk about? Do you talk about sports or what happened at the office more than you talk about God? I want my words to be recorded in the book of remembrance, and I want it to be more than just a line or two.

What is silver? Proverbs 10:20 says, *"The tongue of the just is as choice silver...."* The good things you say to people will make it beyond this life. Taking the time to encourage and build up people will last for eternity. These types of things can handle the flames of fire.

Faith's Hall of Fame

When Jesus appeared to me in 1987, He talked to me about the last days. He said that the working of miracles and the gift of faith would be in operation. He told me that

judgment was coming to the earth; but before the judgment, there would be a time of mercy.

Jesus told me to warn people that judgment was coming. I said, "Lord, I don't want to do that. People don't like to hear about judgment." He said, "It doesn't matter what you want to do, you do exactly what I tell you to do."

In 1990, I was in Hastings, Michigan, staying at the home of a friend. I was in his office listening to a Sandy Patti tape and getting ready for the evening service. The presence of God was so strong in that room that I began to cry uncontrollably.

I looked up, and Jesus was standing in front of me. He never said a word. He didn't have to. He had a look on His face that said, "You better obey me." Talk about getting your life straightened out in a moment. I thought, *No problem. I'll do it.*

I did not do what He told me to do in 1987. I had begun to warn people to a certain degree about the coming judgment and preached a little bit on the working of miracles, but obviously not to the degree that I should have.

I should have been bolder. I was young then, and I thought that young preachers shouldn't be that bold. I've gotten over that. I have some gray hair now, and I am much bolder.

After Jesus had disappeared, I noticed a book in the office by E.W. Bullinger, titled *Great Cloud of Witnesses in*

Hebrews Eleven. This book is about the saints, the great cloud of witnesses who watch us from heaven. I began to read about the people in the Bible who could see afar off.

Today, they are in a heavenly grandstand cheering us on. Their deeds are recorded in Hebrews 11. They weren't blind but could see down through history. Their beliefs caused them to act.

Enoch was one who saw beyond the day in which he lived and prophesied about the end of times. (Jude 1:14,15.) By faith he walked with God and was translated because he pleased God. (Heb. 11:5.)

By faith Noah warned the world of things not seen as yet, and built an ark to the saving of his house. (v. 7.) Abraham saw afar off. He knew he was a stranger and a pilgrim walking on this earth. He was looking for a city whose builder and foundations were made by God. By faith Abraham sojourned to a strange land. (vv. 8-10.) These men saw beyond their present circumstances.

Jesus also saw afar off. Because He did, He was able to endure the Cross for the joy of seeing you and me follow after God. (Heb. 12:2.) If Jesus was willing to die for us to secure our salvation, surely we can endure adversity while we are here. Surely, we can take up the slack and do some things for God.

Being Wholehearted for God

God called each of us before the foundations of the world. We all have a job to do. He wants us to demonstrate to the world His good works. He doesn't want us to be wimps, but to be like these men and women who stepped out in faith to obediently do what God told them to do.

To help us out, God set in the church the five-fold ministry gifts, *"For the perfecting of the saints, for the work of the ministry, for the edifying of the body of Christ"* (Eph. 4:12). The word *perfecting* means "maturing."

When I was a child, the Lord used to say to me, "Walk before Me and be thou perfect." I thought, *I can't be perfect. I'm just a kid.* I did not understand that it meant "to mature." It also means "wholehearted."

The church today is not wholehearted. They are not even halfhearted. If we were halfhearted, we would have had revival twenty years ago. We are probably only a "quarter" hearted.

When you are serving God wholeheartedly, you will find out what He wants you to do while you are on the earth. There is nothing more fulfilling than doing something for God. If you are agitated all the time and are hard to live with, it's because you are unfulfilled. You are not doing anything for God.

God wants us to be assets and not liabilities for the kingdom. We don't want to be dead weight. We should not have 25 percent of the church pulling the weight. Everybody should be doing something.

Filling a Need

About 20 years ago a young man was sitting in the back of his uncle's church listening to the pastor ask for a man to volunteer to work in children's church. The children's church had a group of kids who sat together and were often disruptive during the service. The pastor was looking for a big man to help keep the kids under control.

Even though he didn't feel "led" to work with children, the young man volunteered anyway. He knew if he didn't raise his hand, his uncle would appoint him for the job. That is how Willie George got started in children's ministry. He was filling a need.

You may say, "I don't know what I want to do. I really don't feel led to do anything." Great. If you don't feel called to anything in particular, then look for a need in your church and take care of it.

Be a problem solver, not a problem creator. This is how you will get started in doing the greater works we are commanded to do.

Letting Go of Weights

One time I was ministering at a four-day campmeeting. During the meeting, the host pastor had a minister's luncheon. As I was walking into the meeting room, I was only thinking about the food. I was hungry, and it smelled good! When I stepped inside the room, I had a word of knowledge in the form of a vision.

I was in the back of a boat watching a pastor ski. He was slaloming like a pro. Then I heard the voice of the luncheon minister preach on Hebrews 12:1, *"...let us lay aside every weight, and the sin which doth so easily beset us, and let us run with patience the race that is set before us."* That was the end of the vision.

I continued into the meeting room and sat down at a table. The food was great, and I was having a wonderful time of fellowship. When the minister got up to speak, he said, "Turn into your Bible to Hebrews 12:1."

I thought, *I bet God wants to get something over to that pastor.* After the minister had finished his message, the host pastor said, "Joe, do you have something?"

I went to the podium and said, "We all need to examine our lives and lay aside every weight and sin that holds us back. I have things in my life that I need to let go of. They are not sin, but I do not want to have that type of weight on me. I want to be able to run the race that God has set before me without anything holding me back. Let's bow

our heads and take a moment to examine ourselves and make a commitment to make adjustments in our lives."

As the ministers were praying, I was watching the pastor I saw in the vision. I wanted to see what he was doing. After the luncheon, I went up to him and asked, "Have you been waterskiing lately?" He told me that he hadn't been skiing lately because he has been too busy. I thought, *Oh okay, I missed it.*

I drove back to the hotel with the luncheon minister and told him about the vision I had. He gave me a shocked look, and I asked, "What's wrong?" The minister told me he saw the pastor as he was loading up his car to leave. He asked him to come to the meeting that night. The pastor said, "Well, I can't. We're taking a different route home that takes longer. We need to go through a particular town."

One of the men on his staff said, "We're going to pick up a new water ski for Pastor." Then another person said, "Pastor, didn't you get what the Lord was trying to say to us today? Maybe you need to cut back on some of your water skiing." The pastor said, "Jesus would have to appear to me before I would do that."

I thought to myself, *How could he not think that God was trying to say something to him?* The pastor had the written Word of God. Then the luncheon minister preached from Hebrews 12:1. I encouraged the ministers to throw off the

weights that were holding them back. And finally, someone on his own staff bluntly told him that he should cut back on waterskiing.

Why would God go to all this trouble to get something across to him? He wanted the pastor to be able to run his race fast and without any weights that would hold him back.

In the last days, things are going to be accelerated. If you are carrying a lot of baggage, you won't be able to keep up with what God wants to do.

Finishing the Race

God knows what is about to come on the earth. He can see that people need to make adjustments and let go of whatever is holding them back.

If your life revolves around television, you are going to have to let go of some of this weight. Notice that I said, "revolves." It's not a sin to watch TV, but sometimes you need to turn it off so you can spend time reading and studying the Word.

God wants us to finish the race that we have started. If you have things in your life that are keeping you from obeying Him, then you are tied down with weights. Like Martha, you're overly occupied and have neglected the

important things in life. And that is your relationship with God.

I have never seen marathon runners with things strapped all over them. They want to run so fast that they barely have any clothes on. They don't want anything to weigh them down. God wants the church to be lean and mean. It's time to buffet our flesh and move forward in the things of God.

Get in the Open

When I played football, one year the coach made me the quarterback. I had played split end, linebacker, and defensive end. The year they made me quarterback, we lost just about every game. It was horrible!

If it was midway through a game, when we would do a pass play, I would fade back and look for the receivers. Before I threw the ball, I would check out the split end, the tight end, and the wing back. I checked out everybody.

Toward the end of the game—at the two-minute warning—when I faded back, I wouldn't look for anybody except the tight end. He wasn't the fastest guy on the team, but he had a knack for getting in the open. When I faded back, I knew that I could throw the ball to him every time.

God has the ball right now, and He is ready to throw it. He is looking for people who have a knack for getting in

the open. They have kept themselves pure and holy and are full of the Holy Spirit. They are ready to be used by God in these last days.

If you are open, God can throw the ball to you. If you are encompassed by weights and sin, He will have to look for another receiver.

Jesus compared the end times to the time of Noah. He said they would be marrying and partying, and some would become lackadaisical in spirit. (Matt. 24:38.) Their lives aren't revolving around the criticalness of the hour.

We can see the same thing in the church today. Many Christians are caught up in their everyday lives and aren't aware of how close we are to the return of Christ.

God is merciful, and He has given us a two-minute warning. It is time to throw off the weights that entangle us and go all out in the things of God.

Conclusion

I want Christians everywhere to catch the vision of living a resurrection lifestyle. It is one thing to hear about it and think, *Yeah, that's really great,* and another thing to actually live it. Can you imagine what would happen if everyone who read this book began to operate in the gifts of the Spirit and allow the power of God to flow through them and not just to them? Just think of the impact that would be made in the world.

James 5:7 says, *"Be patient therefore, brethren, unto the coming of the Lord. Behold, the husbandman waiteth for the precious fruit of the earth, and hath long patience for it...."*

God has had long patience for the precious fruit of the earth to be harvested. He does not want to see anyone perish and spend eternity in hell. You and I are His workmen, and it is up to us to bring in the harvest.

When Jesus ascended into heaven, He did not say, "Okay, guys. You're on your own. Good luck." No, He gave us tools—the nine gifts of the Spirit—to get the job done. I have thoroughly explained how each gift works as

well as given many examples from the Bible and in my personal life.

Now it's up to you. John 7:38 says, *"He that believeth on me, as the scripture hath said, out of his belly shall flow rivers of living water."* These rivers are the manifestations of the Holy Spirit. They are in you. It is your responsibility to prime the pump and let them flow through you.

Naturally Supernatural

To walk in the Spirit will require that you spend time with the Holy Spirit. If you want to get to know anybody better, you have to spend time with him or her. The Holy Spirit is no different. If you want to know His ways, you have to set aside time to fellowship with Him by reading the Word, worshipping God, and praying—both in your native language and in tongues.

In 1980 Dr. Kenneth E. Hagin prophesied that there would come a day when Christians would begin to flow in the supernatural as naturally as a bird can fly in the air and as naturally as a fish swims in the water.

The Holy Spirit said through Dr. Hagin that if you would just give a tithe of your time to the Lord each day— that would be an hour or two that you set aside every day to fellowship with God—then your life would be changed. The prophecy said that if you would do these things then

you would flow in the supernatural as naturally as you breathe the very air.

Doesn't this sound wonderful? Don't you want to get to the point where you will be more conscious of the supernatural than you are of the things that are going on around you?

Walking in the supernatural won't make you weird or goofy. You won't be so caught up in the Spirit that you walk into walls or cause car accidents.

Walking in the supernatural is being so sensitive to the Holy Spirit's voice that you clearly hear Him tell you to go to the Piggly Wiggly instead of Kroger. Then when you're picking up a few groceries, you bump into an old high school friend and lead him to the Lord.

Walking in the supernatural is being moved with compassion when you see a young child who was born blind. It is boldly praying for that child and witnessing the child's eyesight being restored the moment you touch her. Jesus will be magnified in everything we do.

Getting Rid of Blockages

I once heard a minister say, "Make sure you're not a dam Christian." He was saying to make sure that you don't dam up the rivers of living water that God wants to flow through you. Now is the time to let go of anger, bitterness, and unforgiveness. God cannot move through you if you are hanging on to something that happened to you in the past.

Even though you may have been wronged terribly, you will find that if you forgive the person who hurt you, God can not only heal and restore what has been done to you, but He can also use you as a vessel where rivers of living water flow through you to heal and restore others.

It is time to get rid of anything that will keep you back from flowing in the power of God.

Let's emulate the lives of the Apostle Peter and Smith Wigglesworth and be bold in our faith. Why don't you just go for it and be daring for God? As you take that step of faith and begin operating in the gifts, God won't let you down.

Actually, the hard part is on God. You can't heal anybody; only He can. You only have to be the mouthpiece that speaks what God says. You are His arms and legs. As you go where He tells you to go and lay hands on whom He tells you to lay hands on, He will then be able to flow through you to cause great signs and wonders to manifest.

I was in Ontario, Canada, waiting for a friend of mine to begin ministering when two angels suddenly appeared in front of me. It shocked me when I saw them, but I knew they were at the service for a reason.

Conclusion

As the Word was going forth, I knew in my spirit that the angels came to deliver a new heart to someone. After my friend had finished preaching, he asked me if I had anything. I immediately knew what I was supposed to do. I said that somebody was having heart trouble, and God wanted to give the person a new heart.

A woman slowly made her way to the front of the auditorium. She looked as though she was going to die. After I prayed for her, you could see an immediate change. When the altar call was given, she came forward and brought her family. They all gave their lives to the Lord.

The woman had a doctor's appointment the next day. After the doctor reviewed her EKG, he asked her what had happened to her. The EKG showed that her heart was perfect. She told him where she had been the night before and how two angels brought her a new heart. After she left his office, the doctor called the newspaper.

The front page headline read "Angels Bring New Heart to Woman." That night, we could barely get in the building. The place was packed with people who wanted to get healed. The meeting was glorious. Not only did people get healed, they also got saved.

That is what this is all about. Making yourself open for the power of God to flow through you to make an impact in the lives of the unsaved. It's time for Christians to get

out of their comfort zone and step out in the power of the Holy Spirit.

We are in the final sprint of a long marathon. Many great saints have run the race before us. They are now cheering us on from the grandstand in heaven. Can't you hear them saying, "Come on. You can do it. It's not that hard. Don't quit now. Just a few more steps, and you have finished the race."

I'm excited about what God is going to do through you in these last days. The lives of many will forever be changed because you were bold enough to allow the Spirit of God to flow through you. There will be great cause for rejoicing at the banquet table of the Lamb when many last minute guests arrive.

The time is short, and what must be done must be done quickly. We are in this together, and together we can make a mighty impact on the kingdom of God. Let's start experiencing some heaven on earth.

Prayer of Salvation

God loves you—no matter who you are, no matter what your past. God loves you so much that He gave His one and only begotten Son for you. The Bible tells us that "...whoever believes in him shall not perish but have eternal life" (John 3:16 NIV). Jesus laid down His life and rose again so that we could spend eternity with Him in heaven and experience His absolute best on earth. If you would like to receive Jesus into your life, say the following prayer out loud and mean it from your heart.

Heavenly Father, I come to You admitting that I am a sinner. Right now, I choose to turn away from sin, and I ask You to cleanse me of all unrighteousness. I believe that Your Son, Jesus, died on the cross to take away my sins. I also believe that He rose again from the dead so that I might be forgiven of my sins and made righteous through faith in Him. I call upon the name of Jesus Christ to be the Savior and Lord of my life. Jesus, I choose to follow You and ask that You fill me with the power of the Holy Spirit. I declare that right now I am a child of God. I am free from sin and full of the righteousness of God. I am saved in Jesus' name. Amen.

If you prayed this prayer to receive Jesus Christ as your Savior for the first time, please contact us on the Web at **www.harrisonhouse.com** to receive a free book.

Or you may write to us at:

Harrison House
P.O. Box 35035
Tulsa, Oklahoma 74153

About the Author

Reverend Joseph Morris travels throughout the United States and abroad preparing the Church for her final hour. With boldness, unusual demonstrations of God's power, and a radical determination to do the will of God, Rev. Morris challenges the Church to use her equipment to bring in the harvest of the last days.

Rev. Morris is a graduate of Rhema Bible Training Center in Broken Arrow, Oklahoma. He and his wife, Linda, and their daughter, Lauren, currently reside in Oklahoma.

To contact Joseph Morris
please write to:

Joseph Morris Ministries
7107 S. Yale
Suite 311
Tulsa, Oklahoma 74136
(918) 296-0440

Or visit him on the Web at:
www.josephmorrisministries.org

*Please include your prayer requests
and comments when you write.*

www.harrisonhouse.com

Fast. Easy. Convenient!

- ◆ New Book Information
- ◆ Look Inside the Book
- ◆ Press Releases
- ◆ Bestsellers

- ◆ Free E-News
- ◆ Author Biographies
- ◆ Upcoming Books
- ◆ Share Your Testimony

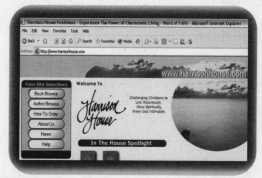

For the latest in book news and author information, please visit us on the Web at www.harrisonhouse.com. Get up-to-date pictures and details on all our powerful and life-changing products. Sign up for our e-mail newsletter, *Friends of the House,* and receive free monthly information on our authors and products including testimonials, author announcements, and more!

Harrison House—
Books That Bring Hope, Books That Bring Change

The Harrison House Vision

Proclaiming the truth and the power

Of the Gospel of Jesus Christ

With excellence;

Challenging Christians to

Live victoriously,

Grow spiritually,

Know God intimately.